*Books by David Schoenbrun*

THE NEW ISRAELIS    1973
(*with Robert and Lucy Szekely*)

VIETNAM:
HOW WE GOT IN, HOW TO GET OUT    1968

THE THREE LIVES OF CHARLES DE GAULLE    1966

AS FRANCE GOES    1957

# THE
# NEW
# ISRAELIS

# THE
# NEW
# ISRAELIS

BY

*David Schoenbrun*

WITH

*Robert & Lucy Szekely*

NEW YORK    ATHENEUM    1973

*For Chaim Vinitsky*

*Israel's greatest ambassador of good will*

*Thy people shall be willing
in the day of thy power . . .
from the womb of the
morning: thou hast the dew
of thy youth.*
—Psalm 110:3.

# CONTENTS

# I

# Israel: Facts, Figures, and Fancies

*. . . Thy name shall not be called any more Jacob, but Israel shall be thy name . . . And the land which I gave Abraham and Isaac, to thee I will give it, and to thy seed after thee will I give the land.*

—GENESIS 35:10, 12.

Two out of every thousand physicists in the world are named Cohen, although the Cohen clan totals only two out of every twenty-four thousand people in the world.

No one is quite sure why so many Cohens—the family of the priesthood in Jewish history—should be physicists, or what, if anything, it means. But there is much about the Jews and the Israelis that is astonishing and inexplicable.

Israel is a semidesert land, with few natural resources, but it has attained the highest yield of cotton per acre in the world and the second highest yield of milk per cow, after Holland. The main foreign-currency earner of Israel, a country at war or in a state of siege since its founding, is tourism, an industry which rarely flourishes in troubled lands.

The Israelis want their country to retain its character as a Jewish state, but they are reluctant to return the territories won in the Six-Day War. However, if they retain the territories, then Arabs will total 35% of the population, and, at present birth rates, might account for more than half the population by the end of the century, so Israel will become a state with an Arab majority.*

Israel is a rural, agricultural country with one of the densest urban populations in the world: 13,447 people per square mile, in Tel Aviv. There are no diamonds in Israel but some of the world's most renowned diamond cutters and designers are there. It is a land of deserts and wilderness but exports fruits and flowers to Europe.

The highest place in Israel is Mount Katarina (Har Mōshe), 8,668 feet (in the occupied Sinai); the lowest is the Dead Sea, which at 1,292 feet below sea level is the

* The population of Israel, in terms of the 1967 boundaries, is just over 3,000,000, of whom roughly 2,500,000 are Jews and 500,000 non-Jews, including 350,000 Moslems, 75,000 Christians, 40,000 Druses, and the remainder scattered other religio-cultural groups.

lowest place in the world.

Israelis are getting married earlier and divorcing less. In 1950, the average age of the groom was 30, and the bride 25. In 1970, the average Israeli male married at age 25 a bride of 21½. Last year, seven young men under 19 married brides over 25 and two new bridegrooms over 65 married brides under 25.

There are a lot of Jewish doctors in Israel but a severe shortage of Jewish nurses: one doctor for every 410 people, one nurse for every 1,500. Israelis spend $7 out of every $100 on health services. They see their doctor 10 times a year. There is an available hospital bed for one out of every 130 citizens, one of the best hospital-service ratios in the world.

The average Israeli male lives to 70, the average female 73, and, as one Israeli wit added, "The average Prime Minister eighty. If you want a long life, go into politics."

The birth rate is 32 per thousand, the infant mortality rate 18 per thousand. The main cause of adult death is heart and vascular disease: 230 out of 100,000.

About 600 Israelis are killed annually in car accidents and thousands are hospitalized. But only 15% of Israelis own cars. If peace ever comes and Israelis can divert moneys from tanks to cars, the slaughter could be awful.

Israelis, particularly young Israelis, are movie buffs. They go to the movies an average of 18 times a year, but that is a statistical average. If one excludes from the figure those who do not go to the movies, then those who do average about 45 sessions a year. The figures, however, show signs of a decline since the advent of television. The average annual attendance in 1950 was 29; in 1967, 26; and in 1970, 18.

Israeli television began broadcasting on regular schedules after the Six-Day War. Before then, only 3% of the people owned television sets. The percentage is now over 50% for Jewish families, but only 14.3% for non-Jewish families.

People have more television sets than telephones; only 35% of the population have home phones.

From 1960 to 1970, ownership of home gas ranges increased from 59% to 86% for all families of Israel.

Electric refrigerators jumped from 47% to 90%.

Washing machines from 16% to 43%.

An indication of the extraordinary literary drive in Israel is found in the fact that the biggest best-sellers of all books were children's books: 4,400 trade copies sold per title, plus school textbooks, 4,700 copies sold per title. About 2,100 books are published annually in Israel, with an average sale of 2,900 per book. There is one newspaper or periodical for every 5,800 people, one of the world's highest rates of print journalism.

There are 12 art museums but more than 30 archaeological museums out of a national total of 95 museums.

Practically every citizen of Israel listens to the news on radio several times a day: 96% of the men, 90% of the women. The reason is grim: announcements of raids and casualties.

There are 11,500 policemen in Israel, one for every 250 citizens. Crime figures indicate that the police are either very efficient or there isn't much crime in Israel.

In 1970, there were 46 charges of murder and 43 of attempted murder, less than occurred in just one week, in August, 1972, in New York City. In all the United States, there was a murder every 30 minutes, according to FBI figures issued in August, 1972; that is a total of 48 murders a day, every day.

All cases of offenses against morality, including rape, came to 2,230 for a population of more than 3,000,000. In the United States, in 1972, there was a rape every 13 seconds.

Israelis have been concerned about the increased use of drugs. Their crime figures indicate that, happily for them, they have had little to contend with: 1,663 cases, including "soft" as well as "hard" drugs.

There was a big increase in house-breaking and burglary in the past decade: from 4,110 cases in 1960 to 32,753 cases in 1970. That's about average for a week in Manhattan. Sometimes we think we had that many in our own apartment house.

Our favorite statistic of Israel is the total of 4,900 licensed lawyers and only 1,985 prisoners in 1970. Either there isn't enough crime to go around for lawyers or if you have a Jewish lawyer you don't go to jail.

*      *      *

Citizens of Israel take these remarkable phenomena in stride. Joseph, a guide-interpreter, brushed aside my compliments: "What's so remarkable about the Cohens? From Einstein to Oppenheimer, we Jews have produced great physicists. As for tourism in a troubled land, just think a minute. Our frontiers are, it is true, unsafe. But our cities! Jerusalem! The most beautiful, the most historic, the safest city in the world.

"Now take your country, America. A great country, strong. Your frontiers are the safest in the world. But your cities! Terrible what goes on there, with the muggings and the murders. If you want an exciting safe vacation, would you go to New York, or Chicago? No! You come to Jerusalem. That's why tourism is good here. It's logical!"

Joseph's comment was typical of the Israelis' sly, self-deprecating, yet arrogant humor. Even more than the French, they have developed an acute *esprit de contradiction*. If you praise something, they tell you of all the disadvantages you failed to observe; if you criticize anything in Israel, they offer a dozen examples to contradict your argument.

There is only one safe generalization that can be made about these highly individualistic people, and it encompasses their intense love of nation, the fervor of their nationalism, and their determination to defend Israel against all enemies and at all costs.

This commonly shared attitude can be found in all classes and among all political groups—officialdom, industrialists and merchants, workers and students—of all ages, from extreme right wing to extreme left wing, with the very minor exception of the most orthodox sects, who refuse military service and even refuse to recognize the existence of a Jewish state until the Messiah comes to save Jews and the world.

Most Israelis think the Messiah would be happier to find a Jewish state in existence to welcome his arrival. And if the Messiah, awaited for thousands of years, still takes His time about salvation, Israeli citizens will at least have lived in their time in their own state, under their own laws.

The Jews of Israel today are the first Jews in some nineteen hundred years to live under Jewish law and Jewish culture. In Israel, Jews are not obsessed with Jewishness. They are people whose religion is Jewish.

Ask an American Christian what he is and most likely his answer will be "Why, I'm American." Ask most American Jews what they are and they are likely to reply, "Jewish." Not that they feel or are less American, but that Jews have so long been discriminated against or persecuted, so long been told they are a people apart, that when one asks them what they are they are almost conditioned to reply "Jewish."

Stop an Israeli and ask him what he is and he will reply either "Israeli" or "lawyer," "storekeeper," etc.

A rabbi from Chicago visited Israel recently and came back singing its praises and its wonders. When I asked him what struck him most, he replied, "I walked down the Dizengoff in Tel Aviv and could not believe my eyes. I saw riveters, street cleaners, barbers, policemen, and firemen. I never saw so many Jews doing Gentile work."

Leonard Bernstein expressed the same sentiment differently: "What's particularly wonderful about Israel is that it proves that all Jews are not violinists."

Jews are people in Israel, just like other people. Good and bad cohabit. More often, which is human, good and bad cohabit inside the same person, depending on pressures, ambitions, circumstances. There are few, if any, Jewish characteristics among the Israelis. The dominant traits and attitudes are Israeli, not Jewish. The food is not Jewish. You cannot get a decent Jewish salami in Israel. The cuisine, like the civil code, derives from the British mandate. The laws are good, the food is terrible, as in Britain.

There is an old joke, which used to be told years ago among Jews, that has finally become a truism in Israel today. It tells the story of the Jewish merchant touring the Far East to buy goods for his shop in New York. He found himself in Shanghai the day before the High Holy Day, Yom Kippur, and discovered that there was a sect of Chinese Jews in the city. He presented himself to the rabbi and asked to be admitted for the ceremonies, offering to make a contribution to the synagogue, which is customary. The rabbi refused to let him pay and welcomed him to join as an honored guest.

At the end of the ceremonies, the rabbi asked the New York Jew if the services had pleased him, and then asked if he might put a personal question to him. When the New Yorker assented, the Chinese rabbi asked, "Are you really Jewish?" The New York Jew, surprised at the question, assured the rabbi that he was. "Well, all right," said the rabbi, "but you don't look Jewish."

In today's Israel, a lot of Jews do not look Jewish; that is, not like the stereotype of a Jew that has become a world caricature. Some eyes slant, as in Shanghai, and some do not, as in New York. Many noses are hooked but they are just as likely to belong to an Arab as to a Jew. Many Israelis are short, stocky, and swarthy, just like Greeks, or southern Italians or other Mediterranean peoples. There are red-headed, blue-eyed Israeli Jews, dark-skinned, sinewy Jews from Yemen, Jews from Morocco and India, from Russia and Brazil.

The Jews of Israel are a mongrel people, in the sense that French historian Seignobos once wrote, "We French are mongrels, a *brassage* of races, which is the source of our strength and ingenuity."

In the course of some two hundred interviews for this report on Israel, one answer surprised and delighted us most. It came in a conversation with a twenty-five-year-old farmer in a kibbutz in the Beit Shan Valley on the frontier with Jordan, a sector that had known much fighting and guerrilla warfare.

We asked the young farmer, "What does it mean to you to be Jewish?" He blinked, frowned, thought a minute, and said, "I'm sorry, I do not understand your question. I am Jewish; so is everyone else. What should it mean?"

In the world outside Israel, most Jews instantly understand a question about the meaning of Jewishness. Only in Israel does one find many Jews who simply take it for granted that they are Jewish and do not think about it.

The young farmer knew what suffering was. He sat on his tractor but had an Uzi submachine gun slung over his shoulder. He had not known one minute of peace or safety in his twenty-five years of life. Until the age of thirteen, he had slept underground in the farm's collective shelter for the children. But he looked upon his struggle essentially as a national struggle, a fight for independence and security, for his physical existence, but not a fight for his soul and his faith.

In this he was different from his father and mother, and very different from his grandparents. It was an interest in these differences that led over the years to this particular book on the new Israelis; that is, the generation born and raised on the soil of Israel since Israel came into existence as an independent state in the spring of 1948.

The young farmer's grandparents emigrated from Russia at the turn of this century. They were part of the generation of David Ben-Gurion, of Golda Meir and Chaim Weizmann. These were the founders of Israel, the visionaries who came to build a Jewish homeland in the ancient land of the Hebrews. They were conscious of being Jews, something special; they knew what it meant to be Jewish in the Pale of Settlement in Russia, in the ghettos of Warsaw, Bucharest, of Vienna, Munich, Paris, and London. They would have understood our question and discoursed on it for hours.

If you had asked Ben-Gurion or Weizmann or Golda what they were, they would have replied "Jews" or, perhaps more likely, "Zionists." Never would they have said "Israelis," for there was no Israel when they came to Palestine. They came, as immigrants, to create Israel one day.

The saga of their struggles is one of the greatest epics of Jewish history, as remarkable as any in the Bible. It ranks surely with the great human stories of a people's struggle for independence.

The generation of the elders of Israel settled on land that no one else wanted. They drained the malarial swamps and reclaimed new land. And they bought land from absentee Arab landlords. Slowly they multiplied and extended their holdings and their families by giving birth to a new generation in Palestine and by immigration from the ghettos of the world.

For fifty years, they labored and they fought and they begged and, seemingly indestructible, they survive today, in their mid-eighties and mid-seventies, as leaders of the land they dreamed about. But emotionally, culturally, psychologically they are not fully Israelis, any more than George Washington, that English gentleman, was an American.

Working with them are their sons and daughters, sharing

their dreams but developing their own brand of toughness and realism, and their own hybrid culture, a blend of their parents' European heritage and their own Palestinian experience. These are the men and women the world knows as the "sabras," the sunburned, muscular farmer-soldiers, the Moshe Dayans and Yigal Allons who forged the new state with their plows and their guns. But they, too, are not fully Israelis. They are Palestinian Jews of European immigrant parents.

Assaf Dayan, son of Moshe Dayan, was born in Israel. He is a true Israeli, with none, or perhaps few, of the "hang-ups" of his revolutionary father or immigrant grandfather. He is, historically, a new Israelite, the first Jew to live in a Jewish homeland since the ancient Israelites nineteen hundred years ago.

These new Israelites are the first Jews in that long span of history not to know what it is to live as a minority or in a ghetto. They know about slums; they have them in Tel Aviv and in Jerusalem. They know about injustice and inequities. Israel is not Utopia, although its standards of social justice rank among the highest in the world. Deprivation, underprivilege, even prejudice are not unknown in Israel. But no one suffers from any of these plagues of man because he is Jewish. For a Jew, this is a change as marvelous as the escape from Egypt.

This change has been accompanied by many other dramatic changes, with consequences yet to be foreseen.

For the first time in the young history of Israel, twenty-five years old in the spring of 1973, the young outnumber the old. Fifty-five percent of the population is under 30, according to the census figures of 1970.

The largest single age group is composed of children, those 15 years and under: 28.6%.

The next largest, the subjects of this report, is the group 16–29, the future leaders of Israel, with their own culture, their own psychology, way of life, and politics and world view. They represent 26.4%.

Those approaching or entering the middle ages, at the peak of their physical and intellectual powers, the group from 30 to 44, represent 26%.

Add up the still-youthful adults, the youth, and the children, and they represent 81% of the present Jewish population.

To be sure, the patriarchs and matriarchs are still the leaders of Israel. At the age of eighty-six, in 1972, David Ben-Gurion was still writing and oraculating in his sun-baked cottage in the kibbutz at Sde Boker in the Negev. He casts his thunder and lightning upon occasion over the Knesset, the Parliament of Israel.

In her mid-seventies, Prime Minister Golda Meir chain-smoked, drank coffee nonstop, insisted upon being called at all hours of the day or night if any soldier or citizen was killed or wounded in combat or an act of terrorism. She treated Ben-Gurion as a beloved and revered older brother, to be kept out of management of the family as much as possible, and looked upon Dayan with affection, pride, and a Jewish mother's disciplinary eyes, as my son the General. And she kept Dayan, Allon, Sapir, and all other Presidential hopefuls guessing as to her eventual retirement and her choice of a successor.

So indestructible and majestic have Israel's founders been that Dayan, entering his sixties, has long been a "young hopeful" in the leadership generation. Strong, vigorous, Dayan is nonetheless an aging grandfather, in the upper ranges of an age group totaling only 12% of the population. The Ben-Gurion-Golda Meir age group, those over 70, represent only 7% of the citizenry. Obviously, they are no longer representative of today's population in Israel.

There is nothing like a rebellion, or even a significant protest against their leadership. One hears occasionally the cry

"Golda, back to the kitchen!" (Women's Liberation has yet to make serious inroads to Israeli politics or society.) But Golda still wins every popularity poll with 80% and more approval of the conduct of her office.

This does not mean that the 81% of the people under 45, or the important youth group from 16 to 29, accept her leadership without serious questioning.

In the summer of 1972, important political groupings came into existence demanding that the government in Jerusalem define clearly its policies on Arab territories under Israeli occupation and on the rights and status of Arab citizens of Israel, going so far as to assert the right of the Palestinian peoples to a state of their own, a very severe challenge to the Prime Minister's views.

The young and the maturing citizens of Israel are restive, rather than rebellious. They are seeking a greater voice in affairs, both public and private. Their restiveness is nothing like the youth movements in America, but it is growing and growing rapidly. Great changes are impending in Israel in the decade ahead.

Although it may well be the generation of Dayan, of the original Palestinian sabras, that succeeds its parents, the Zionists, the children of the State of Israel are going to play a vital, perhaps a decisive, role in four major issues being debated in Israel today:

1. Israel's role in the Middle East, its relations with the Arab countries and the achievement of peace, by far the most profound preoccupation of the new generation coming of age.

2. The aims, objectives, organization, and political and sociological structures of Israeli society.

3. A most explosive question: the place of religion in the state.

4. Finally, the dramatic, human challenge of continued mass immigration into Israel, the controversy over Zionism

and relationships between the Jews of Israel and the Jews of the Diaspora, the world outside Israel.

Neither Golda Meir nor her immediate successors will determine the final answers to these questions. Of course there are no final answers to questions posed by society or world politics.

The new Israelis when they come to power are not likely to determine forever the nature of the state in which they were born and raised. But since they are Israelis born and bred, with less of the traumas and doctrines of the past to influence them, they may have a better chance, thanks to their fathers' and forefathers' magnificent achievement of a dream, to find their own Israeli reality.

Who and what and how many are these first Israelis to come of age in the State of Israel?

What are their family and cultural origins?

How do they break down into social, professional, and educational groupings?

What is their way of life; what are their ambitions? What are their views not only on the four great issues but, on the personal level, their views on love, sex, marriage, a woman's role, politics, work ethics, travel, amusements, food and drink?

How do they live and what are they like?

How do they relate to their parents and their parents to them? How do they relate to Jews outside, particularly American Jews who play so great a role in Israeli affairs?

We put these and many more questions to some two hundred young Israelis and also to their teachers, parents, political leaders, army commanders, and to scholars of Israeli universities.

We checked our samplings against the far more extensive national studies conducted for the government and the universities by the Israeli Institute of Applied Social Research in

Jerusalem. Scholars of that distinguished institution were most helpful in running through their computers the national samplings and extracting and analyzing the answers of citizens in the age group we are exploring.

We will let them talk for themselves through transcripts of the interviews we recorded in the summer of 1971. Since we are reporters and not recording machines, we will also comment on what we saw and thought as well as on what we heard.

What matters most, of course, is what the new Israelis have to say about themselves and the times and circumstances in which they live, in which we all hope to go on living, a hope which cannot but be influenced considerably by what they say and do.

# 11

## New Towns, New Jews

*. . . And they shall build the waste cities, and inhabit them. . . . And I will plant them upon their land, and they shall no more be pulled up out of their land which I have given them, saith the Lord thy God.*

—AMOS 9:14–15.

THE clink of ice cubes being put into the glass brought the promise of cool relief from the searing heat of the African sun at high noon. The waiter poured a pale green liquid onto the ice and it frothed up milky-white when water was poured over it: the traditional French Mediterranean apéritif—*pastis*, a pungent, licorice-flavored alcohol.

The bright red awning over the café tables gave relief from the relentless sun which baked the village square. Two teen-age girls, wearing miniskirts that barely covered their round hard rumps, went by with a roll of brown thighs. The butcher stopped sucking a bleeding finger and stared longingly at the girls. His shop, next to the café, sent over breezes of refrigeration scented with the spice of sausages he had been stuffing. In the center of his showcase was a long rack of lamb, garlanded with mint and roses.

The rolling "rrr"s of Edith Piaf's throbbing voice filled the square: "*. . . me prrrend dans ses brrras . . . me parrrle tout bas. . . . Je vois la vie en rrrose . . . C'est lui pourrr moi, moi pourrr lui, dans la vie. . . .*" The waiter put down a saucer filled with tiny hard black olives and thin slices of red pepper dipped in olive oil. "*Monsieur a choisi? Au menu aujourd'hui, nous avons gigot aux soissons.*"

How many slices of leg of lamb with white beans had I eaten in a quarter of a century of reporting trips to Morocco, Algeria, and Tunisia? How many times had I heard Piaf's "La Vie en rose," "Mon Légionnaire," "L'Accordéoniste" echoing nostalgically of Pigalle across a sun-baked African plain? Dressed meat and roses, sugar-coated *sablés*, raspberry tarts and *religieuses* (the two-tiered cream puffs which irreverent Parisians, in their colorful argot, call "nun's farts").

It was a familiar bittersweet scene, bitter because of the cruel memories of the colonial wars I had reported there, sweet because over the years I had come to love Africa, its multicolored dawns and sunsets, its purple hills, its endless patient defiance of all conquerors. In Africa, one knows that in the end all is shifting sands.

I glanced across the table at my family, all busily at work. My wife, Dorothy, was sketching the scene, a cluster of felt pens in her left hand, a dab of bright blue on the tip of her nose, and a smudge of green on her cheek. My son-in-law Robert Szekely and his wife, my daughter Lucy, were head to head on opposite sides of their portable tape recorder, listening to the interviews we had held that morning at the *mairie,* the city hall.

I was the only one not busily working.

I sipped my cool *anis* drink and idly looked around. Across the square, a big billboard on the cinema displayed a man and a woman in passionate embrace. It was too far to read the title. Beyond the cinema, a boy was kicking the dust and hitting, with light strokes, a little donkey burdened with bags of grain.

Out of the shadow of a covered gallery that ran the length of shops around the square stepped a striking-looking couple, very tall, slender Moors. The man, well over six feet, but looking much taller because of a high red fez atop his head, wore a long white embroidered dashiki over tight cotton slacks that bell-bottomed on leather sandals. A golden loop dangled from his left ear. His wife, almost as tall as he, with large black eyes flashing out of a café-au-lait-tinted face, stood straight under the harness over her shoulders, balancing her baby on her back. A tall, twisted-silk turban raised her almost to her husband's eye level. Just behind them came a group of Indians, the men in turbans and Nehru jackets, the women wrapped in gossamer saris, gliding soundlessly in gold slippers.

I turned to Dorothy, to call her attention to the people in the square, and said, "You know, nobody is going to believe that this is Israel."

This was the new town of Dimona, created out of literally nothingness in the heart of the wilderness of the Negev. It was a miracle of planning and human engineering, the grafting of cultures.

The Indians in their Nehru jackets and saris are Jews and citizens of Israel, immigrants from the small sect of Jews who had found exile in India centuries ago and had now returned to the homeland of their ancestors. Culturally, they are Indians. But their religion is Jewish and their nationalism is Israeli.

The tall, handsome Moors are not Moroccans, not Arabs. They are Americans from Chicago, one of a group of two hundred calling themselves Black Jews, who had first emigrated to Liberia seeking a black life, then to Israel proclaiming themselves to be Jews, descendants of one of the most ancient tribes. The government in Jerusalem opened its doors and its hearts and told them they were welcome. As one official told me, "I don't really think they descend from our tribes, and frankly they are not very Jewish. But anyone crazy enough to want to be a Jew is a Jew."

The French butcher who dresses his lamb in mint and roses is not a Frenchman. At least, he is no longer a Frenchman. He says he never really was. "I am a Jew, born and raised in Morocco. I thought for a long time I was a Frenchman, but in Morocco a Jew is a Jew. Both the French colonials and the Arabs reminded me of that often enough. Not true anti-Semitism. Nothing virulent. No, no, not that. Just that a Jew is not a Moroccan or a Frenchman in the colonies. So I came to Israel and now I am what I am; I am myself."

The new town of Dimona was founded in 1956, as a modern planning development completely different from the original concept of the collective village, the kibbutz, or the cooperative commune, the *moshav*. The scorched plains and rocky hills of the Negev did not lend themselves easily to agricultural development.

The site was selected for good communications with Tel Aviv to the north and the Dead Sea potash mines to the east. Power lines were laid down and light industry located there.

The first families selected to pioneer this new frontier town in the Negev were chosen from Moroccan immigrants who had lived in the mountain regions and would find the topography familiar and be able to cope with the challenge of creating a community in the wilderness. There were thirty-six families in all who set off to found Dimona. They were given tents, water wagons, tools, grain, and twelve chickens each, with the promise that trucks from Tel Aviv would bring them fruit, vegetables, all essentials, and construction teams to build their homes.

From that small start in 1956, Dimona had grown by the summer of 1971 into a prospering city of 30,000 souls. More than half the population were 18 or less, making it the youngest city in Israel. Its birth rate was 4.3%, almost 50% above the national average, assuring its continuing status as the city of youth.

The town "elders," who run the municipal council, averaged 35 years of age. Mayor Navone, who came as a child from Rabat, Morocco, was 33 years old; Vice-Mayor Peretz, who came from Casablanca, was 34. The average age of the 30,000 people of Dimona was 21.

With a town so young, blooming so quickly, it has been difficult for housing to keep up with proliferation, but by dint of a tremendous effort construction did just manage to keep abreast of the human wave. Under these conditions, housing is strictly utilitarian. There is neither time nor materials for luxury decoration. But there are no huts or hovels in Dimona, no slums, virtually no serious crime, no problems of crowding or public hygiene. It is a stunning achievement.

In the early years, each family was allocated sixty-eight square meters of living space; that is, roughly eleven meters long by six meters wide, or, in American terms, about thirty-six feet by twenty. Not a lot of space for a big family—and North African Jews, like North African Arabs, tend to have a lot of children. They also, in compensation, learned how to make maximum use of every foot available. They did not feel cramped in their small quarters, mainly because they had balconies and large windows, and because, as throughout the Mediterranean world, they lived in the streets from sunup to moondown.

As the years went on, the government helped them build additions and extensions to the old flats, while increasing the allocation of space in new constructions. It has gone up to eighty square meters per family, or roughly thirty-six feet by twenty-four feet, a good-sized space even for a large family. Almost all the flats are purchased by the inhabitants. In the past two years, the state and the banks have been granting long-term, low-interest mortgages.

New immigrants get financial loans, outright grants, and tax-exempt status for the first three years, until they are safely established as self-supporting members of society. It is one of the most remarkable, efficient social welfare systems in the world, geared to jobs and self-support.

The credit can be equally divided between the Israeli government and the world Jewish community, particularly the American community, which, in the United Jewish Appeal campaign—philanthropic contributions in the form of cash grants—and the State of Israel Bond sales—investment capital—raised close to a billion dollars for human development in Israel in the past year and a half.

The generosity of the American Jewish community and the gratitude of the Israeli recipients were illustrated at the entrance of a new school we visited in Dimona, the Edith Lehman School and Community Center.

At the entrance to the building, against the wall, is a plaque in the form of a tree. On each branch of the tree, in bas-relief, are sculpted leaves and on each leaf is the name of a donor. Each leaf represents a minimum gift of $1,000. We counted a hundred and eighty leaves on the tree. The names ranged from Edith Lehman—former First Lady of the State of New York, widow of one of America's finest citizens, Governor Herbert Lehman, who, when he was Senator from New York, was the first man in the Senate with the courage to get up and denounce Joe McCarthy—to Dorothy Schiff, publisher of the New York *Post,* down to donors of very modest means, such as the teachers of a junior high school in the Bronx and a grammar school in Richmond, etc.

Sixty new kindergartens and day-care centers were under construction the day we toured Dimona. But there are still four hundred to five hundred young children on the list waiting to find a place in the new schools. The "lag" is taken care of by the fact that in large families there is always an older child to help look after the smallest ones. Seven out of ten families in Dimona might be classified as large: five members or more.

Taxes are light in Dimona, as in all new towns, to encourage settlers, but Israelis are the most heavily taxed people in the world. Anyone in Israel who earns more than $350 a month pays 64% of earnings above that sum in direct income tax. Over a certain amount, an Israeli is taxed up to 85% of his income. In addition, there are many indirect taxes, on imports, sales, fuel, tobacco, alcohol, foreign travel, and dozens of other levies.

A middle-class family in Israel pays twice as much income tax as its American counterpart. For example, a family man with a monthly income of $800 pays 19% marginal tax in America, whereas an Israeli's tax on this income is 37%. The breakdown of income and deductions from the salary of a woman in an administrative job in a nursing home showed the following results:

| | |
|---|---|
| Gross monthly income | 1,040 pounds ($230) |
| Income tax | −240 pounds |
| Voluntary loans to the government | − 50 pounds |
| Social Security | − 40 pounds |
| Net income | 710 pounds |

She is in the low-middle income bracket, yet she takes home just over two-thirds of her salary.

Her cost of living is very high. If she wants to buy a Sony transistor radio, it will cost 77 working hours. A television set costs 555 working hours and a Volkswagen 5,160 working hours,* which may explain why only 15% of Israeli families own a car (all of which seem to be traveling at breakneck speeds on the road between Tel Aviv and Jerusalem). One of the joys of Dimona is that there are very few cars, partly because no one can afford them, partly because they are not needed.

Dimona is a small town, the streets spacious, laid out in patterns that permit easy communication. The weather is pleasant, people are young, lively, and used to walking, and there are good bus communications to Tel Aviv if anyone wants to visit the big city. We breathed heavily in the humid, gas-polluted streets of Tel Aviv, but breathed freely in the dry, clean air of Dimona, a town we kept coming back to in our months in Israel.

Eight out of ten citizens of Dimona are immigrants, six out of ten of them French-speaking, mainly from Morocco. The others come from India, Eastern Europe (mainly Rumania), and, for the past year, Russia.

* The Bureau of Labor statistics gives the figure of $2.44 an hour for a practical nurse as the U.S. national average.

| | |
|---|---|
| For a Sony AM/FM transistor which costs $20, the work cost is | 8 hrs. |
| For a black-and-white TV set at an average low price of $117, the work cost is | 48 hrs. |
| For a Volkswagen at $2,150, the work cost is | 881 hrs. |

The Russian immigration is the most talked about, most dramatic *aliya* among all the waves of Jews who have found a new life in Israel. Almost 30,000 came last year and it is hoped that the rate will continue. The American Jewish community has been most active in calling for and paying for Soviet Jewish immigration. As Paul Zuckerman, National Chairman of United Jewish Appeal, put it: "When one Jew in Leningrad is denied the right to live in freedom, then we, too, are in chains. And when one Jewish child in Morocco must beg for food, it is we who are humiliated."

No Jewish child, and there are many, from Morocco begs for anything in Dimona. Every Russian immigrant is free.

Not many Russians go to Dimona now. The city authorities and the government in Jerusalem believe that 30,000 is the optimum figure to provide homes and jobs for all in Dimona. If it grows bigger, it will suffer the problems of a big city. Besides, it has few resources of its own. Almost all the food and household needs must be brought in to Dimona. It has a thriving textile plant that provides jobs for most of the citizens, in addition to the Dead Sea works which also provide jobs.

There is a high percentage of intermarriage between Rumanian-Jewish immigrants and the Moroccan-Jewish immigrants. They arrived in the same wave of immigration in the mid-fifties. The Rumanians speak a Latin tongue and pick up French very easily. One does not find the Ashkenazic-Sephardic problem in Dimona—that is, the social conflicts between Jews of western, European origin (Ashkenazim) and Jews of eastern, Afro-Asian origin (Sephardim).*

Those who came as immigrants in their teens still tend to speak French, although they have all learned Hebrew by now. The young ones, who came before their teens, or who were born in Dimona, all speak Hebrew by preference, although

* For a full report on this basic social conflict of Israel, see chapter IX, pp. 155–176.

they understand French and will speak it if pressed. Cultures tend to survive even the most dramatic changes of geography and social pressures.

Some seventy years have passed since the great turn-of-the-century immigrations to America, yet grandchildren and great-grandchildren of the Russian, Polish, Hungarian, and Italian immigrants still have some knowledge of the mother tongues. Dimona is likely to look, sound, and feel like a French-Moroccan town for a long time to come. There is strength in this kind of diversity if it can be maintained without conflict.

The Israeli government, while insisting upon the attainment of high standards of Hebrew by all citizens (Hebrew is a vital unifying element of the Jews from a hundred different lands who have come to Israel), also provides for foreign-language instruction at an early level of primary education. There are very few Israelis in the world—three million out of three billion people—and no other people speaks Hebrew, so Israelis must be proficient in the languages of world science and trade.

Fortunately, many Israelis of the older generation are polyglots and pass on their languages to their children at home. In addition, a first foreign language is taken at the fifth-grade level in grammar school and the second in the eighth grade. In Dimona, because of its background, students are encouraged to choose Arabic and French, for which languages local teachers are readily available. In other cities and towns, English and Russian are the most popular foreign languages.

Eli Ouknine, age seventeen, was born in Israel of parents born in Morocco. Even the name Ouknine sounds Moroccan Arab, not Jewish. Small, slender, with curly black hair and olive skin, Eli could easily be taken for a Moroccan. The guttural sounds that accent his French are Arabic. But he is an Israeli Jew, proud to be one, happy that his parents left Morocco in time for him to be born in Israel.

"Israel is like a big family rather than a country. Everybody has a friend or a cousin somewhere in the land. You can move around Israel and always find a place to stay. And we help each other out. There is not the same kind of competition, of pushing and clawing, as in France or in America. At least, that is what my parents tell me. I have never been out of Israel, although I am very anxious to travel."

Almost all Israelis, like Eli, are eager to see the world. They love their own land and say they would not live anywhere else, but they are conscious that Israel is very small and the world rich with new experiences.

"When I finish my army duty, I will go to Morocco," Eli said. "I want to see what it was like there for my parents. They tell me it is a very beautiful country, a fertile coastal strip, high snow-covered mountains. I want to see the wonders of the great bazaar, the Djemma el Fna, the snake charmers, the miles of souks, the dunes of the Sahara, the Blue People. It must be fascinating.

"Then, I want to go to France for advanced studies. My brother is there now, at the University of Marseilles. He tells me that in France everyone is on his own; it is a very lonely place, no sense of community. I would not like that, but it would be useful to study there. French culture is a great world culture.

"What do I want to study? Psychology and psychiatry. The study of the human soul. My friends all laugh at me. They say leave my mind alone. Some even say it isn't Jewish. They're crazy. Was not Freud a Jew? I have already read Freud and books about Freud. This will be my career."

Eli's father was a teacher. He is now pensioned off but helps out in the educational programs of Dimona. His mother is an executive secretary in the Department of Education of Dimona, at the city hall, in the morning and in the afternoon she is a municipal social worker. She is fluent in Arabic, French, and Hebrew.

Eli told us that youngsters in Dimona start going out on

mixed dates, boys and girls, at the age of fourteen. There is no curfew in his family. He simply tells his parents where he is going and he comes home when he pleases.

Eli grinned and added, "There aren't many places to go in Dimona, so parents always know where the kids are and don't worry. We go to the movies, then to the café for ice cream. We sit around and talk till around midnight. That's about it. Oh, for older kids, there is a kind of night club, a discothèque. Touring repertory companies come by about once a month and we get good theatre. The opera and the Philharmonic come a couple of times a year."

Eli smiled shyly. "The girls like to go steady, the boys don't. But the girls often get their way. I mean, a lot of the kids pair off pretty early. Sex? You don't know the girls in Dimona. No, there isn't much early sex. Well, you know, I'm only seventeen and the girls in our bunch are fifteen, sixteen. Well, we don't do—well, I mean, you know, I guess nothing much happens. Maybe it's different in Tel Aviv. Big city. But in Dimona it's a small town; there's no place to go, no cars. Anyway, that's the way it is.

"Drugs? No, not at all—well, not that I know of. Most of the kids smoke, but not much 'hash,' certainly nothing hard. No, we don't drink. Alcohol is expensive and tastes terrible. Wine? Oh, sure, but wine—that's not really a drink. Wine is food."

Eli told us that both his parents are religious and vote for a religious party. "But not me. I'm not interested in religion, except as part of psychological studies. Oh, I do not offend my parents. I am respectful and follow their practices and rituals at home, but it is not part of me. But, of course, I am Jewish. I will marry a Jewish girl, an Israeli girl. We will keep a kosher home, but that is family tradition. I want to be a part of that tradition.

"Politics? It bores me. I pay no attention to it. Maybe that will change later. Right now, I am very busy with my studies,

I'm preparing to go into the army. I have no time for politics and no interest in it.

"What kind of girl do I want to marry? That's a funny question. How can I tell? Well, in general, she shouldn't be ugly, at least not uglier than I am."

Eli's white teeth flashed and lighted up his face. "I wouldn't like my wife to be smarter than me, or have more education. Or maybe that would be all right, if she would have me. Why not? She should be what she is and do what she likes. If she wants to work—okay, work. If she wants to raise a family, then that's fine.

"I want a good family, but not so big as my parents have had. We are nine brothers and sisters in our family. That's great for the kids; we all felt very happy and secure with all our brothers and sisters. But it was tough on Mother and Father. Me, I'd like a family of about four kids, no more than that.

"How to control it? Well, there's safe abortion, if necessary, but I don't like the idea of abortion. It is really killing, isn't it? But now there is the pill; that is preventing not killing. My girl friend and I have talked about it. Yes, we talk about marriage and kids and sex." Eli laughed, "Now, remember, I said we *talked* about sex."

As we left, we congratulated him on his sense of well-being and happiness. Eli looked surprised. "I'm seventeen, have enough to eat, love my family and my studies, feel fine. Why shouldn't I be happy?"

We smiled and let it go; any comment would have been either fatuous or cruel.

\* \* \*

Dimona is the outstanding example of hope, faith, and general satisfaction with life in Israel. But this is not equally true of all new towns. There are great differences apparent in a nearby town, Dimona's so-called twin city of Arad less than twenty miles away in the wilderness.

Arad is not at all an identical twin, except insofar as both cities were built out of nothingness in the bleak, arid Negev.

Where the population of Dimona is Sephardic—of North African origin—the population of Arad is almost exclusively Ashkenazic. Almost all the settlers are immigrants or children of immigrants from Russia and Eastern and Central Europe. The social strains between these two groups through Israel are readily apparent in the human laboratories of Dimona and Arad, for although they are geographically separated, with no competition to put strains upon them, there are nonetheless sharp rivalries and resentments.

The young people of Arad are generally of a much higher cultural and social standard than the Dimonans, reflecting accurately the national differences between "western" Jews and "eastern" Jews—eastern, in this sense, meaning originating from the Arab lands of the Middle East or North Africa.

Dimonans told us that Aradians looked down on them, were snobs, and felt they were better than anyone else. Aradians did not hide their own pride at their higher cultural levels and tended to "put down" Dimona when we praised it and cited its successes.

Many of the men of Arad work in the district's atomic plant, as highly skilled technicians or engineers, at salary levels very high for Israel; in fact, in terms of net salary, after taxes, their salaries are probably the highest in the country, because of the generous exemptions and fringe benefits awarded to "pioneers."

Technically, they are pioneers in that they came to a wilderness and built a town in the ancient dust and sands of the Negev. But they did not sound like pioneers in our talks with them.

\* \* \*

Zvi Rubin, a textile engineer, twenty-six, born and raised in Haifa, told us, "I came to Arad because I was offered a high salary, a good flat, and low taxes. One day, I'll go back to Haifa, but right now this is a good place to live, work, and put money aside."

His wife, Rebecca, stuck out her tongue at him and said to us, "For him it is a good place to work and live. For me it is the desert. He leaves at dawn almost—he's out of the house, waiting for the bus to Dimona, before six. I've got the baby, housework, and nothing to do until he comes home at six o'clock. And then there's still nothing to do. Gossip with the neighbors. The men play cards and don't even talk to the women. There's nothing to do here. I wish he could find a job back in Haifa."

The difference between Rebecca and the young women we met in Dimona is that Rebecca is a university graduate, raised in a big city. She loves theatre, concerts, cafés and restaurants, going out at night, meeting new people. That is not the life of a new town.

The women of Dimona are less frequently troubled than Rebecca, for many of them came from small towns or kibbutzim and from poor, large families. Having their own spacious flat in Dimona, raising their family with an adequate budget, represents social mobility upward for a poor Sephardic girl, but downward for an urban, educated Ashkenazic girl like Rebecca.

On one level, however, the two cities seemed very much alike, for in this sterile wilderness Arad and Dimona are both blooming cases of human fertility. Or, as co-author Lucy Szekely put it, "This place is a baby factory." As Lucy moved her slim, lithe, as yet babyless body through the streets of Arad, between crowds of ballooning females, she whispered to us, "My God, they make me feel abnormal."

Lucy had unwittingly given voice to a sentiment we later heard expressed by a young mother on a kibbutz: "The first year of married life is very difficult for a woman who has not yet conceived and who is surrounded by newly re-pregnant mothers. The social pressures for conception are terrifying."

Not only are social pressures great, but there are great social encouragements for large families. First, there are the tax exemptions. Secondly, in the new towns, there is an availability of low-cost, long-mortgage housing. One can buy an apartment for a $750 down payment and thirty years of installments at simple interests of 4% and even less.

In Arad, a young couple can not only get a comfortable twenty-by-fifteen-foot room, with kitchen, bathroom, and balcony, but they can change the apartment for bigger space as the family increases from baby to baby. No one is afraid to have a child because of salary or housing, as in Tel Aviv, Jerusalem, or, even more seriously, in Paris or New York. It makes an enormous difference to the security and happiness of youth.

\*     \*     \*

Gabi, aged twenty-four, is a typical Aradian. He was born in Hungary, emigrated with his parents to Israel when he was eight, finished grammar school and a year of university, and considers himself to be a true Israeli, with no real memories or ties to Hungary.

Gabi works as an electrical specialist in the atomic plant. He learned his specialty in the army, as so many young Israelis do. He had a brilliant army career, being one of forty successful applicants out of a thousand for the submarine service of the navy. Submariners are an élite group in Israel, along with pilots, frogmen, and tank commanders.

Gabi is a lucky man, living on borrowed time. He was one of the crew of an Israeli submarine tragically lost with all hands on board—all except Gabi, who arrived late from a leave and missed the sailing of the ship. He was shocked and despondent for many months. He had helped build the submarine in a British dockyard, and the ship and his shipmates were the dearest things in his life.

Gabi is now happily married and well employed at the atomic plant, with a gross salary of 1,800 Israeli pounds a month and a net take-home pay, after deductions, of 1,250 I.£., roughly $425 gross and $300 net, with no rent and with low mortgage payments, health services, and other benefits. "It's a great setup," he told us.

He has every modern appliance in his apartment—TV set, washing machine, refrigerator, electrical stove, vacuum, etc.—plus some sophisticated electrical gadgets and wiring he installed himself. One thing he does not have: books. His apartment does not even have a bookshelf. This is not typical of young Israelis; it is just that Gabi is a tinkerer who loves to use his hands and let his head rest.

His wife, Simka, does not agree that it is such a great setup. She is a middle-class girl from a middle-class home, born and brought up in Tel Aviv. She admits that there are material rewards and advantages in living in a new town like Arad, but she misses Tel Aviv and its bustling life, particularly its shops. She does not read and is not clever with her hands, on which time lies heavy in the wilderness of Arad.

Simka is a strict orthodox, Gabi is not, and that is a source of friction, as it is throughout Israel. Her parents did not want her to marry Gabi, for he was not "observant." He agreed to lead a religious life, and they finally consented to the marriage. He has now cut his religious life down to Friday night services.

Simka is a strong-willed girl and it is a good guess that the family is not long for Arad. Indeed, it is a good guess that many of the Arad families will move on, once they have attained the economic means of mobility. But there are hundreds of applicants waiting to move in, so the future of Arad seems assured, at least as a way station from the desert to medium- and big-city, or—more likely, according to present patterns—suburban living.

\*    \*    \*

Dalia and Yigal are friends and neighbors, living in the same kind of apartment, with fewer gadgets and a lot of books. Dalia only finished high school, but her bookshelves are crowded with much-thumbed copies of Camus, Dostoevski, Brecht, and Hemingway.

She is a bright, outgoing, frank young woman. She told us that several of her friends were pregnant before marriage and that, indeed, the pregnancy was the real reason for the marriage.

"It's fairly common," she asserted. "You'll hear the opposite in your interviews, for most people will tell you there is very little premarital sex. Don't you believe it. We are a decent people, but a lusty one. The Jewish virgin bride is folklore, not today's Israeli." She laughed and added, "Oh, don't think we are promiscuous girls. We are not. But, after eighteen, anyway, 'steadies' find a way to have sex together."

Her husband, Yigal, also works at the atomic plant. Unlike Gabi and Simka, he is bookish, passionately interested in politics and philosophy, and complains that life in Arad is "very limited—few creative outlets."

"We have our work, very interesting work, but our wives have nothing to do but walk the baby, clean the house, and exchange medical remedies for baby problems, and by the time we come home they are up-tight and nervous."

Dalia told us that she had been born and raised in a *moshav,* a cooperative community settlement. Her parents, Eastern European intellectuals, could not adjust to the rural agricultural life of the *moshav.*

"Now I, like my parents, am lost in a desert. This is no life for me. I am not complaining about the wonderful advantages of the new town, or the great social program of the government, and all that was done for us. For some, this is a paradise, but not for me."

\*   \*   \*

We met many in Dimona who thought it was a paradise, and some who thought so in Arad, but many were misplaced there and will certainly leave. This is to be expected in a new town, even though careful screening of applicants was designed to cut down on those unfit. Arad is a boom town, with a population growth, like Dimona's, almost double the national average.

Socially and economically, Arad is a success. Culturally, it must still find itself and find spiritual outlets beyond material advantages for its people. The grim wilderness all around it is oppressive. It is depressing to sit at a picture window or on a balcony and, for miles around, see nothing at all, not even a hill.

The authorities of Arad and of the central government in Jerusalem are aware of the problem and its importance for the future. They are sending touring theatre and opera repertory groups through towns like Arad and Dimona more frequently, and hope before long to have a weekly schedule of theatre, art exhibitions, and concerts.

Programs are delayed by lack of funds, for first priority in Israel must be given to defense, which siphons off almost a third of the national product, and to the basic needs of new immigrants and the heavy social budget of the Jewish state.

# III

# Of Women, Sex, Love, and Marriage

*And Deborah, a prophetess, the wife of Lapidoth, she judged Israel at that time. And she dwelt under the palm tree of Deborah between Ramah and Beth-el in mount Ephraim: and the children of Israel came up to her for judgment.*

—JUDGES 4:4–5.

O F course women are equal to men. Equal in all rights. But you must admit there are many differences and you can't change nature. Women should marry young, raise babies, keep the house. A woman should be the cook and take care of her family. Why? Because that's the way it is; that's the way it should be. Well, sure I said women are equal to men. If they work, they should get the same pay. But can a woman command a tank? Do anything a man can do? No, certainly not. Some things are for women, some for men."

The speaker was not an old man, set in traditional ways. He was a youngster, an eighteen-year-old. His name is Shlomo Havne and we met him, along with a group of young men and women about to enter the army, getting preinduction lectures in Tel Aviv. We spent a week with them, getting their views on a wide range of topics. We will be hearing from them in the course of this report, but at this point we have collated their answers on the questions of a woman's role, of marriage and of sex relations, in the present context of Israeli society.

Israel is a patriarchy dominated by a matriarch. As any man who is head of a Jewish family can tell you, this is not a paradox but a routine fact of Jewish family life. The father figure is the head of family, the brother more important than the sister, the mother everybody's slave except for the fact that family life and virtually every important decision is made by the mother.

Golda Meir is the almost perfect illustration of this matriarchal-patriarchal conundrum. She is admired, even loved, obeyed but not feared, and, beyond challenge, the strong-handed leader of a nation and government not easily controlled. Men like Moshe Dayan, Yigal Allon, Pinhas

Sapir, and Shimon Peres are strong leaders themselves, dynamic and tough, and one wonders about Golda's ability to control them all. Israel would seem to be a natural fertile ground for a Women's Liberation movement.

Telling jokes or stories about Golda is a favorite pastime in Israel. Some of them are unprintable. Some are stories based on truth, repeated with gusto and pride. One tells about David Ben-Gurion's trip to Paris to confer with General de Gaulle and to introduce his new Foreign Minister, Golda Meir.

The meeting went well. De Gaulle could be exquisitely courteous when he chose to be, and Golda can be a good listener when she chooses to be, and both chose these unaccustomed roles for their meeting. It was a good moment, for de Gaulle was then an enthusiast of Israel and a great admirer of the Jewish people. (The rupture of good relations after the Six-Day War was a tragic loss for both.)

Midway through the meeting, Golda excused herself to permit the two men to continue their talk in complete privacy. At that point, de Gaulle turned to Ben-Gurion and said, "Mr. Prime Minister, I am interested in your choice of a woman as Foreign Secretary at a moment of such danger for your country. Does she have special qualities or is there something in your ethics, religion, or mores that gives women a prominent role in your society?"

Ben-Gurion raised his lion's head and roared with laughter. "Golda? A woman? Why, Golda Meir is the very best man we've got. That's why we chose her."

Some time later, in an interview, the author asked Golda Meir if she had heard what Ben-Gurion had said about her, and if she would make a comment for CBS News. Golda smiled and said gently, "You mean he said I'm the best man he's got? Well, you can quote me as saying this: Men think that's a compliment."

In a country led by that kind of woman, universally admired, one might not expect much need of Women's Lib. But as our interviews revealed, Golda is old Israeli, from the generation of the founders, the pioneers, the frontiersmen and frontierswomen. Golda is not the new Israel, and her grandsons and granddaughters hold different views and practice different life styles.

\* \* \*

Shlomo Havne likes Golda: "But I wouldn't want my wife to be in politics. I hate bossy women. Anyway, Golda is not a woman—I mean she is, of course, a mother, a grandmother; I mean no insult—but she is so much more than that. Golda is a monument, Golda is a kind of genius. Who wants a genius for a wife?

"What do I want for a wife? Why, a good girl. She should not be stupid." (Out of two hundred interviews, we must have heard that phrase a hundred and fifty times.)

Shlomo is short, broad, strong, built like a peasant. He is gay, laughs a lot, is sure of himself but not arrogant, with a happy-go-lucky charm, and an easy confidence in his simple views rarely found in an eighteen-year-old.

He was born in Israel of parents who had emigrated from Rumania. His father is a computer programmer, and he has been taking a course at an IBM school while working as a postman since finishing high school, awaiting his army induction. Like every eighteen-year-old we met, boy and girl, he was eagerly awaiting his army service, a phenomenon we have met nowhere else in the world.

"I will get married after I get out of the army and finish my university studies, and get a job, of course. The army service plus university—all that means that most Israeli men can't get married much before twenty-three, twenty-five. I think even that is a bit early. I'll get married when I'm well able to. My wife will, therefore, be a few years younger than I, and probably have less education. Certainly I don't want to marry a better-educated girl. No, that wouldn't be good."

Shlomo locked his hands behind his neck, flexed his arm muscles, and puffed out his chest. He did this several times during our talk; it was a kind of physical tic, probably nothing, but seeming, in the context of his comments, to be a very male gesture.

"I believe that marriage is an important criterion by which one can judge one's ability to take a vital commitment. Marriage should be based on love, of course, but it is also a human commitment composed of many obligations and duties. It also requires a monogamous philosophy. Maybe it is not natural to be monogamous. I don't know. But you can't always just do what's natural or there would be no society. You must build a family, with strong bonds of love and respect. That rules out promiscuity. That requires total commitment. It is a serious business and should be taken very seriously.

"Yes, I agree that many girls are as smart as boys, even smarter. Sure, they are entitled to have a career. Housework is boring, particularly for an intelligent woman. But that's the way it is. Particularly if there are children. When a woman is pregnant, she has to stop working. That isn't easy for the organization she is working in, with women dropping out a couple of months every year. Well, maybe after the kids are going to school, she can go back to a career. That's the way I see it."

And that's the way about 65% of those we talked with, of both sexes, saw it—with variations, of course, accepting more or less freedom and equality for women, but with greater stress on legal and theoretical equality than real equality.

\*     \*     \*

"Marriage is a vital institution; it cannot be done away with, or even altered to any great extent," we heard from Hava Yanay, aged eighteen, who hopes to go to the university to train for teaching languages and the Bible after her army service.

Hava is a very pretty, sexy, long-haired brunette, with a pouty and sulky look. But she has the views and attitudes of a middle-class matron, spiced by a few cautiously liberal ideas. Her parents came from Poland. She was born in Israel.

"How can you bring up children properly without a central, firmly united family group? Only in the family can the child be given a proper moral training, a training for life. School can't do it. And the family must be a good family or it can't do it either. There must be discipline, a sense of responsibility, a sharing of duties and obligations, a sense of each one's role," Hava asserted.

"A career? Yes, I want to be a teacher. That is quite compatible with being a wife and mother. Maybe when the children are very young, I must stay home and take care of them. But I could do tutoring at home. Then, when they go to school, I can teach. It is better for the children if the mother has something to do other than just run after them."

Hava ran her fingers through her long, silky hair, twitched and swished attractively in her chair, sipped an orange juice (only the sophisticated older city set drinks alcohol), and commented: "No, I have not had an 'affair,' if you mean sleeping with a boy, although we are not frigid, you know. To tell the truth, I think it might be a good idea to have a kind of trial marriage; that is, to live with a man before deciding to marry, to get to know each other better. Not just sex, but everything.

"Marriage is important and should not be entered into lightly. It's a problem. I'm not sure just what is best. In any case, such a system would be hard to practice here in Israel, for it is not generally accepted that a man and woman should live together before marriage. They do that, I think, only in the kibbutzim. And I hear that there was a lot of freedom among the early settlers."

Hava laughed, her face lighting up, her natural loveliness radiating through the make-up. "Our grandmothers were real swingers, I guess. We are not."

*     *     *

Shulamit, aged eighteen, was born and raised in a kibbutz. Her family emigrated from Yemen. She is dark, plump, with merry black eyes but a shy manner.

"My dream is to live in Tel Aviv one day. What a big, exciting city! I want to work in an office, meet a lot of boys, get married, and have a lot of children. Marriage is good, marriage is right. You start with love, of course, but hot love does not last. It is then that marriage helps you keep your man from running away."

*     *     *

Shaul, like Shulamit, was raised in a kibbutz. His parents came from Rumania. He did not like kibbutz life: "A man can't be himself there; everything is for the community. I'm going into the army now; that will be better, for the army will give me special training. I am interested in criminology. I think I want to join the police, specialize in the drug problem. I think drugs are very dangerous. Too many of the kids are already smoking 'hash' all the time."

Asked about his views on marriage, Shaul answered, "I want to have the upper hand in marriage. The man should be the boss. Women's Lib? That's a lot of nonsense. Women have more freedom than men. They run the family affairs from day to day. The man works and gives his wife all the money. Still he should be respected as the head of the family. That's what I mean by he should be the boss. I don't mean a slavemaster. Housework slavery? What are you talking about? That's nonsense.

"Yes, we are different from the older generation. Our parents were Zionists, fired up by faith. Most of the older people were very idealistic and many of them very ideological— you know the kibbutzniks, the socialists, all that. We are more down-to-earth, more hedonistic. Why should we be all fired up about Zionism? We were born here. Israel is our land. That's enough—why shout about it?"

\*     \*     \*

These eighteen-year-old conservatives proved to be highly representative of their peer group but by no means representative of the full youth group, from eighteen to twenty-nine. We found more sophisticated views on love, marriage, and the woman's role among those in their mid-twenties, among the young marrieds and those just approaching the "adult" turning point of thirty. But the percentage of those, even the more sophisticated, who regard marriage as a basic institution of society, who frown upon radical ideas on sex-relations, and who are highly mistrustful of the Women's Lib movement remained high at all age levels.

\*     \*     \*

Edna Weizman (no relation of the illustrious family of similar name) is a slim, short-haired brunette, neat, trim, and poised in her uniform of a lieutenant in the army of Israel. "I am not a fighting soldier. Women should not be fighters. But I serve my country usefully and contribute to its security."

Edna, at twenty-three, has a variety of jobs in the army. She is a supervisor of girl recruits, an organizer of clubs and group trips, a teacher and lecturer in psychology for young soldiers. One of the courses she gives is entitled, "Self-Identity of the Soldier." She is a graduate of Hebrew University, with degrees in sociology and history.

"The principal role of women in the army is to free men to do the fighting," Edna asserted. "There is another role, which you must not misunderstand. Let me try to make it clear. We are good for the morale of the soldier. In the Sinai, for example, or in other wild front-line encampments, a nice girl sets a good example. Without us, the soldier could become a fighting animal. With women around, there is a civilizing influence.

"We are equal to the men in every respect except physical strength and the psychological readiness for combat and killing. In some fields, maybe, we are even better than the men. For example, we are very good at intelligence analysis and at languages. We are better students of Arabic than many of the men. We have a feeling for psychology and social work.

"You think this is not true? That it is a matter of conditioning to believe this, that we are brainwashed? Freud was not a woman, you say? That's very interesting. Maybe you're right. Anyway, that is the way I see it, conditioned or not.

"Most Israeli women do not want to be careerists. They want to marry and raise a family. Many, of course, want to do useful work, too, not just be a housewife and mother. That is very important. But it is different from being a careerist. One can be a housewife and a mother and do useful work. That is good. It is certainly what I want.

"I want at least three children. Who knows, maybe more. After eating comes the appetite. But I would not want to sacrifice my work. I think I can raise a family and teach or do social work. A child needs a mother and a father when it is very young. It is hard for fathers to be home a lot, so the woman must do this at the start. But when the children go to school, we can work, too."

Edna smoothed out her uniform automatically as she thought.

"There is a double standard operating here, I admit. What's right for men is not right for women. Men go to work, women stay home. Men have affairs, women are not supposed to. Men can get away with it, women can't. Yes, there is a double standard. But it is a fact, not a rule.

"What do I mean? I mean that if a woman does not want to accept the double standard, she does not have to. I know women who break it and are not broken themselves because of it. It takes a very assertive woman to act like a man, but it can be and is done. So it is not an absolute rule, the double standard. But it is a fact, in that most women simply accept it and, in truth, are not too unhappy with it."

She paused again. Something seemed to be troubling her.

"I don't like to talk about American society, particularly with Americans who know it so much better than I. But I have studied about American society at the university, and read a lot of American sociology. I think you Americans are very unhappy. Maybe you know too much, or brood too much about what you know. Like the double standard. All right, it's not a good thing, it's unfair. But why such a fuss? A smart woman can get around it. And it works two ways, you know; we get a lot of advantages out of our relations with men. You Americans might get what you want and then hate it.

"The American way of life is materialistic; that is the way of life of the older generation that youth is now rejecting. Well, frankly, I welcome America's materialistic thinking in its sound pragmatism. Where it goes wrong is not so much in the materialism but in making materialism almost an ideal, by worshiping money and things and status. Real materialism, the liking of efficient gadgets, of comfort, of good housing, nice cars, boats—what's wrong with that if it does not become consuming instead of merely consumerism?

"The trouble with American youth is that they not only reject what is wrong in their parents' life style but reject everything, even what is right. How do you say it in English: they throw out the baby with the dirty water."

Edna sought to articulate her views on America. The subject fascinated her.

"Your hippies, your revolting youth, with their pop culture, guitars, the troubadours—we see them here in Israel. Where do they think they are going? How foolish will they be, with their unkempt hair, jeans, and guitars at forty or forty-five? And their marriage ceremonies! Making up their own vows, with a friend officiating. Why, it is a fairy tale, not life.

"They are right to talk of love and peace. They are right

to scorn automobiles and color television sets if they don't like them. But what do they offer? Do they contribute anything to the world, even to themselves? Have they really found happiness? No, I don't think so.

"It is better to live with rules and make the best of them. It is better to respect tradition and respect institutions such as marriage. Life is not a fairy tale, but it need not be a nightmare, either. This is what I think and most of my friends think so, too.

"Oh, we have Israeli hippies, and smoking of pot, and troubadours. But not many. Army training, the need to defend Israel—this does not leave much room for such things."

\* \* \*

Ishaiu Rodoy rose through the ranks to become the commander of a group of thirty men in the air force. Born in 1948, when the State of Israel was born, he considers himself a true Israeli, different from the older generation, many of whom were born and raised in other lands.

"My father was born in Russia, my mother in Poland. They met in a refugee camp in Germany. They will never forget the terror of Hitler, the horrors of the holocaust.\* They did not even dare tell me about it until I was fifteen years old. Many members of our family died in the ovens. Intellectually I can understand the horror but it is impossible for me to *feel* it. That is already a great difference between the new Israelis and the old ones."

Ishaiu said that his generation had its own trauma: the Six-Day War.

"It was a great victory, of course. Had we lost, we would have been slaughtered. Israel is the only country in the world that cannot afford to lose a war. Germany and Japan were rebuilt by the Americans. Even the Russians, with their heavy hand and their police systems, have had to make an ef-

\* For national opinion on this question, see Appendix: Continuing Survey, E1, p. 243.

fort to rebuild the countries of Eastern Europe. But can you imagine the Egyptians, Syrians, and Iraqis rebuilding Israel?

"That is why we fight so hard; that is why no sacrifice is too great for defense. But, let me tell you, we young Israelis who fought and would fight again do not talk about the 'glory' of war. We hate war. I was sickened by the killing even though I knew what I had to do. I fought through the Sinai, the West Bank, the Golan Heights. I saw the stinking corpses, the carrion birds. That's not glory. It is life and death for us to hold off the Arabs. We have, and we will if we have to again. But there'll be no parades, no boasting legions of veterans. That's not us."

Ishaiu puffed on his cigarette, screwed up his face, and said, "You want to know about the role of women in Israel? It's simple: take notes as secretaries until they get married and raise a family. That's about it.

"Sure it's unfair, a waste of talent and lives. Why, I'm studying engineering at Technion and only three percent of the students in engineering are women. You know why? There's a prejudice against women in engineering, and women are constantly told it is 'man's work.' That's not true; it is not man's work. Girls are brilliant at math, physics. They can do the work. But they are pushed into being secretaries, servants to men.

"Even the army, which is very democratic and education-oriented, and gives women officer ranks readily, shunts them off to 'women's work.' I met my first girl friend in the army. She was a marvelous person. We talked about politics and life and she was highly intelligent. But all everyone kept telling her was 'Find a husband, get married.' "

We asked Ishaiu whether this could not be changed by political pressures.

"Yes," he said, "I suppose anything can be changed by political action. But although I think it is unfair, I would go slow about changes. It is a kind of Pandora's box. What demons will be let loose by a Women's Lib program? Gradual change is best. It will have to come from the women themselves." He grinned. "Frankly, we men are not going to campaign for it."

We asked him to describe his ideal girl, in real terms; that is, the criteria he had established for the kind of girl he wanted to marry.

"That's easy to answer. I've thought about it a lot. First, she should be a good girl. Second, she shouldn't be stupid. Third, she should have a good education, but not too good— that is, she does not have to be a university graduate or have advanced degrees. Finally, she should like me; we should like each other, but we don't need total devotion. *La grande passion* does not necessarily make a good marriage."

Among peoples as evolved and diverse as the Israelis, there is no single national "type"—probably there isn't anywhere— but Ishaiu Rodoy's views, particularly on women and marriage, certainly represent the very large majority of the new Israelis. At least seven out of ten of the young men and women we talked with expressed similar views.

\* \* \*

Israeli author Amos Elon, in his brilliant, insightful study *Israelis: Founders and Sons,* asserts that young Israelis are not romantic, not sentimental, and are cool in their relationships. He cites letters from soldiers to sweethearts without a note of tenderness or an expression of affection, to say nothing of love.

We asked all the interviewees what they thought of this observation. One of the best answers we heard came from a twenty-two-year-old girl in Arad, who patted her swollen belly, kissed a baby in her arms, and said, "We must be doing something right."

Most young Israelis said that Elon's observation was quite accurate on the surface but that his generation (Elon is in his mid-forties) simply did not understand the new generation.

"It is a matter of style, not of substance," said Rebecca Riesner, age twenty-one. "We do not articulate as the older ones do. We do not prattle on about love or write love poems or love letters. That is simply not our style. But we court in our own way; we love in our own way. Human nature does not change. All that changes is different ways of doing the same thing."

\*     \*     \*

Gabi and Nava, both twenty-one, sociology students and army interviewers in psychology, whom we met in Jerusalem, disagreed on love and sex.

Nava, good-looking, well-groomed, dark-haired, conservative in style, could be comfortable in any Middle America setting. Her general outlook would not surprise any "silent American." She claimed that "all the girls and most of the boys will identify the twin relationship of sex and love. You can't make love without love. That is what animals do."

Gabi laughed. "Am I an animal, Nava? I can make love without love. A real pleasure to see a pretty girl. You don't even know her and you think, Well, with that one . . ."

Nava flushed angrily. "Yes, you are an animal. I, too, can look at a boy and say to myself, 'That one . . . I'd like to know him.' But even if I had sex fantasies, I would not want sex until I knew the man, found him compatible in other ways. A woman needs an emotional and also an intellectual attachment, not just sex."

"No, no, Nava," Gabi said, "do not say that is what a woman 'needs.' What you mean is that is what you have been conditioned to think. Your education, your environment, your family upbringing—so many factors bring pressure upon a woman to see sex and love as inseparable. But I doubt that this is a biological truth.

"Women are more frustrated about sex than men, but a normal woman has the same sex drive as a normal man. However, she has been trained to defend her virtue, to put a high value on her love. Then, too, women are always more worried than men about pregnancy—they do the carrying, bring up the baby. This is inhibiting to an unmarried woman. Societal taboos and penalties are very severe on unwed mothers. That is the truth, and it has little to do with so-called 'needs.' "

Nava did not at all like the way the conversation was going. She frowned and flushed and fidgeted.

"Yes," she said, "conventions are important, as are taboos and penalties. But there are human differences between the sexes. Boys look at and think of certain female character-istics. We do not concentrate on male characteristics. I don't care whether a boy is handsome, so long as he is not down-right ugly. We girls look for 'man' in all the aspects of man-hood. Sure there are supercharged girls, but I'm talking of the average women I know among my friends and in the army, and for us sex and love are one and marriage is the consummation.

"Listen, I wear light clothes in the summertime, but I do not bare my breasts, even on the hottest days. That is a submission to convention. Well, marriage is a convention, too. I would not live with a boy without marriage."

Gabi laughed. "You're telling me!"

He reached over and squeezed her hand. "Yes, convention is strong, and our generation—we are not rebels. I, right now, am not ready for marriage. I'm only twenty-one. But I ad-mit that in a few years I'll be ready and accept marriage as a true commitment. One must live by laws. Children need par-ents, a family context. Even if I wanted to live with a girl, I can't conceive of bucking my family—how my mother would carry on!—her family, our friends. It's easier to get married. Society makes you give in in the end, so why fight it?"

*     *     *

Aliza is twenty-eight, unmarried, lives with her parents in a typical Moroccan family group, with five brothers and sisters.

She was born in Israel, finished high school and one year of university, and works as a clerk in Tel Aviv.

"I don't care what anyone says, men need sex more than women. Frankly, I suspect they want it more than they need it. The movies, fashions, books, everything seems designed to stimulate—overstimulate the sex urge. There is a constant sex battle between boys and girls. It's hard to watch the movies and a boy's hands at the same time.

"I was very nervous about sex as a teen-ager, of course. Most girls are. Nervous and eager, fighting ourselves. Well, now I am twenty-eight, that's different. Yes, I am planning to get married. Maybe a trial marriage first. There's nothing wrong with that if it is with a steady man and the object is marriage. I am against promiscuity and so are almost all my friends. I can't speak for all of Israel, but there is no free-and-easy sex in our circles. Some sex, yes—we are normal— but no sleeping around.

"I am not religious but I am opposed to divorce. Marriage laws should be very strict and it should be difficult to get a divorce. That stops hasty marriages and broken homes. There ought to be more sex education in the schools, particularly in high school for teen-agers. And we need some education on population control. We have too many big families and too much encouragement for big families. I would favor easy abortion laws for women with three children or more.

"I approve the drafting of women into the army, but they should not be used for combat, should not do any fighting. Why? Because a woman is a woman. Girls don't make good soldiers. They lose their heads easily. I saw this lots of times when I was in the army. Equal rights, yes, of course, but with recognition of the differences between the sexes."

*     *     *

As we listened to our tapes and collated the answers to our questions, we understood just why Amos Elon, and many other intellectuals in Israel, do not find the new Israeli youth "inspiring," and why the bulk of his book on the founders and the sons was devoted to the founders, not the sons. Authors Lucy and Robert Szekely, educated in New York in the turbulent sixties, during the height of protest movements by students, women, blacks, were stunned by the new Israeli youth in the early weeks of our exploration.

But as the weeks went on, as we began to know the Israelis better, to understand the context of their society, to look at them through their own eyes, not ours or their elders', to dig beneath the surface, we saw the pattern of a strong, stable, healthy young generation. If a big part of life and liberty is the pursuit of happiness, then the new Israelis are well up in the race, despite all the burdens of defense and taxes that they must bear.

Health is less dramatic than sickness, a conformist less interesting than a rebel. But there is a radiance to health and a strength in conformity if coupled with intelligence and drive, as they unquestionably are in the new generation of Israelis. As a sociology professor at Hebrew University put it, when we asked his view of the new Israelis: "After fifty years of trailblazing by Ben-Gurion and Golda and Dayan, it is perhaps time to settle down and consolidate the gains."

# I V

## College Without Youth

*Take fast hold of instruction; let her not go: keep her; for she is thy life.*

—PROVERBS 4:13.

T H E sun was furnace-hot and the quadrangle of the university was a flagstoned desert. But spread over the green lawns, under thick-leafed trees, were clusters of bright human flowers, in red and yellow striped shirts and blue jeans. You could tell the girls from the boys easily enough. The girls had short-cropped, curly hair, the boys long locks and heavy beards. With its bright sun, tree-lined walks, modern white buildings, and open arcades sprawling over a wide space, it looked very much like any campus in southern California. It was the Hebrew University in Jerusalem.

We had an appointment with the editors of *Lillit*—Queen of the Evil Spirits—the college literary and political periodical. But first we would be meeting with a young teacher of political science, Zvi Hagadi, who was working on his doctorate and whom we had met on the Columbia University campus in New York.

Zvi is an Israeli, born in 1947, of parents who had emigrated from Poland. He had worked on his thesis on comparative governmental systems briefly in Paris and New York. He was a member of Siah—the New Left movement in Israel—and was familiar with its French and American equivalents.

"The first thing you should know about us," said Zvi, curling his beard with his index finger as he spoke, "is that we are really fundamentally different from the French Maoists or the American S.D.S., particularly the more militant and violent wings of those student movements. We are intellectually militant, not physically. The true fundamental difference, however, is that we disagree with our government, criticize our society, but are not alienated from it. Alienation, that is the key difference, a vital one.

"The New Left in Israel is a very small minority of the

country, even a small minority of the student body. But since we are highly educated, go on from the university to jobs in key sectors, we are more important as an influence than mere numbers would indicate.

"Almost all Israeli youth finishes primary school and a very large percentage—eight out of ten—now finish high school, or an equivalent trade and technical school. This is a high percentage of literacy and education, which will have an increasing effect as the years of education accumulate.

"Education was not so important in the generation of our fathers. For men like Dayan, high school seemed enough. They were brought up by pioneer parents. Zionists and utopian socialists, with a mystic faith in the nobility of the soil, of a closeness to earth. They were doers, rather than thinkers. That is, our parents' generation. Our grandparents, the early founders, the forefathers of Israel—they were intellectuals and great talkers, exalted, almost fanatical.

"We are not like that at all. Oh, we talk a lot at the university—you can take that as intrinsic to university life. But we are more pragmatic, career-oriented, urban, and if we burn about any glory, it tends to be literature or science, not closeness to the soil. Our strength in agriculture is agricultural research—we have the best schools in the world, and we send our best students to study in the best universities in the world, particularly your magnificent American institutions."

Zvi laughed and added, "That's where we picked up a lot of our notions about opposition to the government and criticism of social institutions.*

"We have seven major institutions of higher education, with about forty-five thousand students. Our students are much older than yours, because of the three years they spend in the army before coming to the university. Our average freshman is twenty-one, twenty-two. He is, therefore, much

* For national opinion on this question, see Appendix: Continuing Survey, C3, p. 240.

more mature than his American or French equivalent, less inclined to militancy, anxious to make up for the three years in the army, thinking of the job he wants to get, the girl he wants to marry.

"There is a lack of places available in our most prestigious institutions and faculties, such as medicine, biochemistry—the 'life sciences'—and engineering. Candidates for entry outnumber places in the ratio of 1.3 to 1.8, which is not too bad when one considers that in the last twenty-two years the university population has multiplied exactly twenty-twofold!

"We have five thousand scientists doing 'R and D'—that is, research and development—in the civilian sector, and much more in the military sector. We are very advanced in physics, with a number of outstanding nuclear scientists. Our Hadassah Hospital has one of the finest medical and surgical staffs in the entire world. And, of course, the whole world respects our Technion, the engineering school in Haifa, and the real jewel of our research crown, the Weizmann Institute in Rehovoth.

"Eleven thousand foreign students have come to study in Israel in the past decade and we have sent twenty-six hundred Israeli specialists to teach and guide other countries in their specialities."

Zvi began to twirl his curly sideburns, and laughed.

"I suppose you are wondering what kind of a New Left rebel I am? Pretty nationalistic briefing I'm giving you, eh?

"Well, I am, it is true, very proud of my country. We have done wonders, wrought miracles here, and I want you to know it. But that doesn't mean that all's for the best. It isn't. We of the New Left have real complaints, and we mean to push them, to militate for change.

"The most important is peace. We think our government is hard-line,* that not nearly enough is done to explore every avenue of peace, to offer real sacrifices for peace. We don't

* For national opinion on this question, see Appendix: Continuing Survey, A4, p. 235.

need to hold the Sinai. Perhaps a bastion at Sharm-el-Sheikh, in the high ground, something minimal. We cannot and must not annex the West Bank. We should be pushing for a Palestinian state, not against it.

"We are not blind fools; we know the dangers and we are the soldiers who fought when fighting had to come. Our parents don't grumble about the 'pleasure generation' any more, not since we showed what we were prepared to do in 1967, in the Six-Day War. Now the older generation has to show us what they are prepared to do, for if they fail, we are the ones who will have to fight and die again."

Zvi waved his hand and pointed to the young men and women sprawled around the campus, sipping orange drinks, kissing, playing guitars. "You're looking at the world's best civilian soldiers. Best educated, best motivated. But they want no more of it. They want peace.

"Next, we want social justice for all. And freedom, total freedom. We must end class, ethnic, and religious differences among Israeli Jews. And we demand a hundred percent civil rights for Arabs, Christians, and non-Jews of all kinds who are Israeli citizens. If there are inequalities of a basic nature—such as big families among Afro-Asian Jews, lack of a work ethic, cultural lag—then these inequalities demand a special additional social effort on their behalf.

"It's no good to say, 'These people won't work,' or 'These people won't study; they won't pull themselves up.' That is an evasion of the problem. Educational and psychological programs must be doubled so that half of the population does not continue year after year to fall further behind the other half. That is the major problem of Israel.

"It has been complicated by such fools as the [Israeli] Black Panthers and their more fuzzy-minded supporters, launching the accusation of discrimination, expressing resentment of Russian immigrants—why, that's absurd. The government does not practice discrimination and the Russian immigrants are not the cause of the problem; they are only part of the problem.

"The government has tried. But not enough. That is our main argument." *

Zvi looked at us, laughed again, and said, "Not very 'left' as a position? Well, not in American terms perhaps. I suppose we are 'liberals.' But everything is relative and we are the 'left' of Israel—except, of course, for the minuscule communist group, one not to be taken seriously."

\*　　\*　　\*

We left Zvi and made our way into the cool tile-and-stone interior halls, through a dense crowd of students and teachers, everyone munching on a candy bar or sucking a soft drink through straws. As we began to climb up to the *Lillit* magazine offices, we thought of our meetings with Mark Rudd and the Students for a Democratic Society on the Columbia campus, where we were teaching a course on Vietnam, in the turbulent spring of 1968, when American and French universities exploded with fury and were drenched in blood. Hebrew University in Jerusalem seemed a haven of peace and tranquility. If Zvi was typical of the left, then Israeli youth is one of the most conservative in the world.

\*　　\*　　\*

*Lillit* is published in English, aimed at the large English-speaking student body, the Americans and the British Commonwealth students. For Israeli students, it is an important link with university movements of world Jewry, particularly because Israel, in the Middle East, feels so remote, so isolated from world currents. Nine thousand copies are circulated monthly for ten months of the year, excluding the Jewish New Year and Passover periods.

We met the editors in an office cluttered with papers, crushed coffee containers, littered cigarette trays, and empty

* For national opinion on this question, see Appendix: Continuing Survey, C4, p. 240.

beer bottles: a typical campus magazine office.

Ari Rotem, an Israeli who completed his military service and has studied educational psychology at Santa Clara College in California, is, at twenty-six, the oldest of the editors.

Pamela Lubell, an immigrant from London, is completing her studies in Chinese. She has been in Jerusalem for four years and became a citizen in 1970.

Jonathan Lubell is a sociology major, a "potential immigrant"; that is, he has declared his intention to become a new Israeli but has not decided whether to finish the process.

Judy Bank, from Newburgh, New York, took her B.A. at Albany University, is an American, undecided about citizenship or immigration.

Jochim Herson, in the process of becoming an Israeli, is a Canadian, a student of theatre and graphics.

Ray Goodman, another "processing immigrant," is a South African, studying art history but preparing graduate work in African studies.

At the beginning of the informal "round table," everyone talked freely except Ari, the oldest editor and the Israeli among new immigrants. He listened intently and silently, but when he began to talk, it was with a low-key strength and force that commanded the attention of the others. He sat among them like a rock, being beaten but unmoved by their stormy waves of argument.

Judy Bank started by saying that she had been raised in the World Zionist Movement. Her parents told her that her whole family in Europe had been wiped out by the Nazis in the holocaust.

"My parents became militant Zionists. Only the creation of a Jewish state could save Jews, they said. They were traditional, ethical Jews, not religious Jews, but, they said, 'Make no mistake; for the world, a Jew is a Jew, whatever you think you are.' "

Judy told us that she was made to feel that she could not

be a complete human being, "that is, a complete Jewish human being, unless I lived in Israel. And then America was undergoing so swift, so violent a change that life, particularly for a young student, was difficult in America.

"I came here to Israel in 1965. I was surprised by the strong strains of materialism I found. I guess I expected that Israel would be a utopian socialist paradise. Well, frankly, it was not. I found, too, a very hard line on war, on military security.* I should have expected it, of course, for Israel faces a life-or-death struggle, but you know in America we grow up fearful and mistrustful of the military influence; we hate the war in Vietnam, so we are all dedicated 'peaceniks.' Then to come to Israel and have to kind of switch mental and emotional gears—it's not easy for an American."

Ari spoke for the first time. "That's exactly the trouble with you Americans. You expect too much and you give too little. Dayan is not Curtis LeMay and our fight is for survival, not for political dominance. You must rid yourselves of your preconceptions and learn to take things as they are. And give more—give more of yourself, for you have so much to give. You are bright, educated, spirited. You lack discipline and steadiness."

Ray Goodman, of South Africa, spoke up: "The Israelis have made bad mistakes. You have developed a racist policy. Indian Jews are dark-skinned, so people here assumed they were inferior. They are tolerated as merchants, just as, for so long, the world treated us Jews as all greasy, swarthy, money-grubbing merchants. That this should happen in Israel!

"The Russian and Eastern European Jews made this country, so when they were followed by others, the new immigrants could acculturate easily. But for the Afro-Asian Jew there was a cultural shock. So, again, you assumed they were inferior. You should adjust the culture and politics here to the

* For national opinion on this question, see Appendix: Continuing Survey, D2, p. 242.

fact that a little more than half the country is of Sephardic origin, but there is only one Sephardic Minister, and one Arab sub-Minister in the government. That is discrimination."

"No," said Ari. "That is the result of serious errors, not discrimination. I prefer errors to neglect. We did not neglect the Afro-Asian Jew. We took their children into class with the children of the Ashkenazim. There was no segregation. We assumed they would all learn together and grow up to be the same kind of Israelis. It did not work out that way. We should have discriminated, given them special help, special treatment.

"I do not condemn my parents for their errors. It is better that I work to correct the errors. My parents were not racist. Golda, Ben-Gurion—do you dare to call them racists? You, in South Africa, you know what racism is; why do you bring the charge here? You know, all of you—you bring your angers with you, see us through distant optics. Why do you not just look at Israel, at our reality, and pull together to help?"

Ari ran his hands over his close-cropped hair, rubbed his temples, while his bright gray eyes looked around the table. He seemed to be measuring his fellow-editors, taking care not to let their differences devolve into a heated argument.

"Look, you are right; no one denies that we do have serious problems, particularly since the cease-fire.\* The longer the cease-fire lasts, the more military pressures ease up, so will social pressures increase. No doubt the Zionist model was Eastern European, not designed for the Oriental Jew. It was not right in the fifties; it is not right now. But the strain of conflict can be a positive force for change or a negative force for change.

"We must achieve progress through struggle. That is healthy. I do not want my son to be different, except as in-

\* For national opinion on this question, see Appendix: Continuing Survey, D1, p. 241.

dividual differences are concerned, from the son of an Oriental Jew. There must be one Israel, one people, diverse through personality but all equal under the law, with equal opportunity. We all agree on this, don't we? Don't you believe this is what Golda wants, what Dayan wants, what they are seeking to do, even without enough success?

"We need time. We must have time and patience to learn how to achieve the goals we agree on. And you know that the Oriental Jew in Israel cannot be compared with the plight of the blacks in America."

"Ah, Ari, if Israel is just going to be another state, then to hell with it. It's all the same shit!" Judy Bank exploded.

"Judy, Judy, why are you so bitter, so angry? You come here to us with love in your heart and with stars in your eyes. But you bring with you your own hurts, disappointments, frustrations. Leave them back in Albany, New York. This is Jerusalem, your true homeland. The Promised Land. Sure, I know what you will say: promises, promises. But so many of our hopes have already been realized, promises turned to reality. Why can't you accept that all the promises cannot be fulfilled at once?"

Ira Teitz, a young Canadian, had walked in and listened to the exchange between Ari and Judy.

"Judy is right; it would be a terrible tragedy if Israel just becomes another nationalistic, capitalistic state. Israel is the Promised Land and more is expected of it."

"I am trying to be realistic," Ari said. "I, too, do not want Israel to become a country just like any other, where a man cannot realize his full potential, where there is prejudice, discrimination, with upper classes and lower classes frozen by the system. But that is not happening in Israel. You all look at the current problems and inequities and fail to see the progress that has been made in every sector."

Jochim Herson broke in: "No, it has not happened yet, but it can happen and I disagree with you, Ari. There are signs it *is* happening, the growth of materialism and privilege."

Ari shook his head. "You discount all the new social programs, the new research on disadvantaged peoples. . . ."

"Yeah, more research, less application," Jochim snapped. He leaned forward, his face flushed. "Ari, I envy you and therefore maybe resent you. You Israelis are so self-confident, arrogant, self-assured. I am a Canadian but I lived a lot in the United States, in California. I feel deeply insecure, alienated from today's world. I thought I could find security, faith in Israel. I don't say I won't. I haven't given up. But I am shaken."

Ari smiled, leaned over and put his hand on Jochim's. "So you think we are self-confident, arrogant, smug? What do you know, my friend, of our fears and self-doubts? Simply because we do not articulate them you think they do not exist. You talk of the cultural shock of Oriental Jews in an Eastern European Jewish society of Israel. So let us talk a bit about the cultural shock of you Americans and Englishmen in our society.

"You are used to expressing yourselves. Without offense if I may, you are used to shooting off your mouths. You are self-indulgent and self-pitying. That is not healthy, certainly not for a Jew. It is too easy for a Jew to feel self-pity; we must avoid that pitfall of false pride.

"What you call Israeli arrogance is our outer shell of toughness, of rudeness, like the sabra fruit. Well, we have had a tough life—our fathers, forefathers, our own generation. We have had to be rude and tough. You fellow-Jews who come from other lands, particularly Western lands, you wear your hearts on your sleeves and your nerves outside your skins. You are quick to criticize before you have even understood, before you have made a sacrifice or contribution.

"You know what is the trouble with you Americans, who have so many fine qualities? You have never learned to work from within. You have the complex of outsiders. You stand outside society, look in, hold your noses, and say it stinks. You are quickly alienated. You learn to love your alienation. You think it is a mark of distinction.

"If I love my country, you call me nationalistic. If I serve in the army with pride, you call me militaristic. If I say it takes time to solve difficult social problems, you say I am evasive. Above all, although you shout and scream a lot, you do not see a fight through. You won't stick with a problem to solve it. If you can't wave your wand and make things right, you break it in a rage and denounce society."

The room was quiet, tense with anger, when Ari finished.

"Well, now, I'm sorry. It isn't good to personalize arguments. I meant no offense to anyone. But maybe it has been useful to talk ourselves out, to understand each other better. Come on, let's all have a lot of beer."

Jochim laughed, his anger gone. "It's on you, you materialistic, militaristic—"

"I may be all those things, but I'm also broke, so we all split, okay?"

The editors laughed, crushed butts, got up to go to the cafeteria.

"I hope you won't be too upset by this quarrel," Ari said as he came alongside us in the corridor. "We have pretty lively discussions about everything up in that room."

We laughed. "Teaching at Columbia, lecturing at the New School and at a hundred American and French campuses, has accustomed us to this kind of meeting. Frankly, we thought it excellent; you were all communicating and it made a lot of sense."

We told Ari that we were trying to find out the special characteristics, the identifying marks of his generation of new Israelis, where they were different from or the same as their fathers and forefathers.

We walked along down another flight of stairs, through the main hall, toward the cafeteria as he thought for a long time about our question.

"I think I would say this. The first immigrants cleared the swamps. Their children, along with the second wave of immigrants, made the roads, raised defense forces, created the state. The new immigrants and my generation of Israelis— together we must make a new culture, a new society. I would say that this is our distinguishing task, whatever may be our distinguishing characteristics."

\*      \*      \*

Philippe Rosenau is preparing his doctorate in mathematics at Tel Aviv University. His wife is finishing her B.A. degree. They have been married for six months, hope to start raising a family when they finish their studies and get teaching appointments.

"I vote Herut [rightist party]. I believe in the strongest defense of Israel. We should waste no time arguing about the justification for our being in Palestine. That is a trap for endless discussion, without point. We are here. The U.N. itself agreed on the partition of Palestine. There is nothing to discuss.

"For Jews, there is only one question. Do we have the right to live? There is only one answer. Yes, we do. So let's get on with it.

"Never in history has a people been so generous, so open to brotherhood as we Jews. We want to live in peace with our neighbors. We open our doors to our brothers and sisters of the world.

"America vaunts itself as the country welcoming immigrants, offering a new life, free of religious persecution. But that was in the past. Today America has quotas on immigration. I do not say this in criticism. Let America do what it thinks best for itself. But do not tell us what to do.

"No, no Americans have the right to say that we must let the Arabs come back, unless they are ready to return their own lands to the Indians. Are the Russians ready to return the huge hunk of Poland the Russian bear bit off in World War II? Will the East Germans take back the refugees they expelled? Who are they to give us lessons?

"There are almost half a million Arabs living in Israel quite freely. Myself, I think they ought to leave, for, as free as they are, they are a small minority of Moslems among the Jews.* I do not want to live like that; that is why I'm glad my parents brought me here as a boy from Poland, where Jews could not live a decent life in freedom. If the Arabs want to stay, let them stay. But I think everyone is happier living among his own. If the Palestinians had their own country, they could spend their energies building for themselves instead of the stupidity of trying to drive us out.

"I understand that the Arabs living today look upon us as invaders of Arab Palestine. Historically they are wrong; Palestine is not exclusively Arab. But from their viewpoint, yes, I know how they feel. But we Jews must stand together for our own rights. When they see it is hopeless, when they have a state of their own, then there will be hope of peace. Not before. And, alas, not soon.

"American immigrants do not come here looking for freedom; they have freedom in America. They come either out of frustration with American life or looking for some kind of ideal society in Israel. These are the wrong reasons. They should come only because they want to live as a majority among their fellow-Jews; then they would not be so disillusioned.

"One day, I hope that Israel will have such a society that it will attract people who are not persecuted but are idealists. We are not there yet. But, remember, our government is only just going to celebrate our twenty-fifth anniversary. That's a very short time and I think we have done fabulously well so fast."

* For national opinion on this question, see Appendix: Continuing Survey, A3, p. 235.

Philippe listened to our question and replied, "No, of course I am not satisfied. I know there have been failures. Our government calls itself socialist but it has failed to solve elementary social problems, even educational problems. Take the Afro-Asian slum of Hatikva, here in Tel Aviv. Why, we should pay double the salary for a teacher in Hatikva as against the rich districts of Tel Aviv. We should attract the best teachers to the disadvantaged children. Instead, the children with the best-educated parents, who help them at home, get the best teachers in school.

"The pretension of equality is at the root of our social problem. Everyone may be equal under the law, but not in social and psychological terms. We should recognize the difference between equality in theory and equality in practice, between de-facto and de-jure freedoms. That's our problem. I think many other countries, even the freest, have the same problem."

*    *    *

Yitzhak was born in Israel and his parents were born in Palestine, a family of old settlers. His father works in the post office. He is taking his degree in economics at Tel Aviv University. He is twenty-four.

"Maybe it's because we came a long time ago, but I do not believe in Zionism. Zion exists and we have a tremendous job to make our Jewish state strong and viable. Waves of immigration are very troublesome, costly, a great burden now. This sounds selfish, but nothing is more important now than strengthening the state.

"The Arabs get more help than Israel. They get help from Russia and the United States both. They get help and arms from the French. They have oil billions. The U.N. is pro-Arab and anti-Israel. We have had some help from America and American Jews, for which we are grateful—vital help. But we have had to do most of the work and fighting ourselves against terrible odds.

"I vote for the Gahal Party. I think we should keep most of the territories, keep the Arab guns as far away as possible.

"Yes, there are classes here that are disadvantaged but also there is great social mobility. They should study and work harder instead of complaining and looking for handouts. Like some of the new immigrants, too.

"No, I don't oppose the program of *aliya;* I support immigration, but at slower rates and with less special privileges."

\* \* \*

Esther, at twenty-five, is a dental student. She came to Israel from Casablanca when she was seventeen. Her French is better than her Hebrew. She is a militant in the Civil Rights Movement for Sephardim.

"Our system here in Israel makes no allowance for Oriental culture. It is all European-based. Perhaps that is necessary to some extent, for European culture is more modern, but it is overemphasized and not enough allowance is made for cultural lag and cultural shock, affecting more than half the population, which is of Afro-Asian origin.

"Since so many Afro-Asian Jews are dark-skinned, while Europeans are lighter-skinned, we begin to see an outline of racial distinction coincidental with class and cultural distinctions. The government denies this. My fellow-students deny this, but it is the simple truth. Look around you; you will see how they cluster in groups, how they segregate.

"Yes, true, it works both ways, the Sephardim also tend to segregate themselves, but mainly because they have not had the special training they need.

"No, that's all that interests me. I care nothing about politics itself. No, no, the civil rights movement and my dental studies—that's already a lot."

\* \* \*

Beni was born in a Nazi camp. Somehow his parents survived, kept him alive, and brought him, as a baby, to Israel in 1948.

His father had been a farm manager in Galicia, in Poland. His mother ran a grocery store. They both work now for a grocer. Beni is in the army but taking courses for his degree in history.

"I finished my army service but signed up for another three years because the army is financing my education. Without the army, I would not have an education; that is, a university education. It is wonderful what they do for us.

"Of course I'm a student. Why do you ask? Oh, being in the army does not stop me being a student. They help me study. Not a student like normal students? I guess not, if you mean doing nothing but going to class. But you know many young Israelis do not only go to class. We are not professional students.

"I am religious. I go by the Bible, for religion and for history. I hope to teach classical Jewish history.

"I vote Gahal. Many of my friends do. Maybe next time I'll vote Avoda, a government party. One has to be realistic, support the government, push it in the direction one wants. We cannot afford a severe split. We must be united.*

"Golda does a good job. She's a juggler. Keeps all the balls in the air, lets nothing fall.

"What we need most is an unequivocal guarantee from America that you will not let Israel go down. We'll do the rest.

"Israel may be in the Middle East, but our future is with the West."

\*    \*    \*

Iliezer, twenty-two, is taking his degree in law. He is an Israeli, born and bred, third generation of his family born in Palestine, then Israel.

"You want to know what we're really like? We're what you call 'square' in America, and we don't think it is an insult.

* For national opinion on this question, see Appendix: Continuing Survey, C2, p. 239.

"The American kids, they'd die if they thought they were square. Nonconformism is the new American conformism. They make me sick.

"I've smoked 'hash.' Don't like it. Don't like whisky, either. Awful taste. I know there's a lot that's wrong, but I can get along. I can make my way. If everybody did the same, we'd be all right."

* * *

We sat in the garden, in the cool of evening, in the graceful home of Amnon Rubenstein, Dean of the Law School of Tel Aviv University. His handsome brunette wife, Rowena, had made a fruit punch and was suggesting a "spike" of vodka. It was too hot a day for any alcohol, so we gratefully filled up on the punch alone as we told of our experiences in Jerusalem.

Dean Rubenstein, a fit-looking man in his early forties, is a well-known columnist and television commentator, a cultured, witty, well-informed man about Israel.

"Well," he said, "as so often is true in a discussion of that kind, they all were right and all were wrong. Foreign criticism is very helpful but, as is natural, is always resented. That's why Ari said, 'Why don't you make a sacrifice, a contribution before you shoot off?' But, it's good for us to listen to new immigrants. That is how our society will continue to improve itself.

"Among youth, they can work it out. But it gets more passionate between the youth and their parents, the youth and the government. There is certainly a generation gap here in Israel. It is composed of many factors.

"Peace and war, this is the major issue. Those who must do the fighting should be listened to, and I agree that our government has, in many sectors, a hard line. But Ari is right when he says that the new immigrants, particularly from America, carry a special chip on their shoulders—a kind of passionate attachment to their own alienation.

"We don't have that kind of alienation here—not at all.

Maybe our biggest danger is the opposite. You will surely find a good deal of conformism amongst Israeli youth. The majority is more like your own 'silent majority' than like the S.D.S."

Rowena Rubenstein came back to the garden carrying a platter with a big pitcher and tall frosted glasses. It was one of the few Israeli specialties we loved; most of the time they served salted nuts, cheese crackers—everything to make you thirsty and hold the water until you felt you would burst of bloat. This was iced coffee, filled with balls of ice cream, a joy in summertime Tel Aviv.

"My students are, to a degree you do not have in the States, career-oriented, serious, pragmatic, and, to put it bluntly, very square," said Dean Rubenstein.

"It is not easy for progressive Americans to relate to them. They are intelligent, excellent students, mature, and hard-working. But they are not sufficiently curious intellectually. They are not trained for free discussion and argument as they are in American universities. Sometimes you look at them and see row after row of inkwells that you are pouring facts into and that they pour back into exams. That is not very inspiring for a good teacher. It's our own fault. We ought to make changes in the early educational process."

The Dean thought a moment and ate some ice cream.

"We have had a turbulent history. We have lived with crisis. It is inevitable, I guess, that a new generation comes along that wants normalcy. That could be healthy, but on one condition. It's something that worries me. If they are pragmatic, that's one thing. But if they are indifferent, that's something else. I'm not yet sure where the majority is going, to a cool intellectual, responsible politics—fine!—or to a material acquisition of goods and comforts, leaving the affairs of state to others, in search of the middle-class bourgeois life for itself; then, not so fine. In fact, that would be tragic.

"I cannot agree with the student who said, 'If Israel is going to be just another state, then to hell with it.' After all, this is my country, how can I say the hell with it? But there is something very important in the thought that Israel must not be 'just another state.' No, it must not be and it is not.

"I hope the young generation will not forget the origins of this country. We do not ask them all to be Chaim Weizmann, Golda Meir, or Moshe Dayan. They don't want to be heroes. Fine! We have enough heroes. But Israel is a hope, a promise, an example, and it would be tragic to lose this. I do not think we will."

\*    \*    \*

We asked to meet a student leader at Tel Aviv University and were told to start with Yoel. The friends who recommended Yoel had a suppressed smile but would not explain why. We discovered why when we met him.

Yoel has dark brown hair, a thick beard, is very fat, active, noisy—the type known as "irrepressible." He is twenty-seven years old, getting on a bit to be a student leader, even in Israel where students are older.

Yoel is a student organizer. When we asked what he organized, he said, "Well, everything, but my main concern is organizing immigration of students to Israel and caring for new immigrants when they come here."

We were surprised. This was not exactly what we thought student organizers did. Later we met many other student activists, concerned about politics, social affairs, course-orientation, college reform, the kind of issues that motivate student activists in other countries, although not in the same numbers or with anything like the passions on campuses in the Western world. Israeli students are very different from their counterparts elsewhere.

Yoel began by giving us a dissertation on Israel's right to be in Palestine. We told him we had gone into that thoroughly on other levels and wanted most to hear from him, as a student leader, the principal interests and concerns of Israeli students.

"We are most concerned about our borders; that is, how to get peace on our borders. Everyone will tell you peace is the first concern. But there are many arguments on how to achieve it and what our borders should be. I think, and the majority of students here think, that we must keep Jerusalem and the Golan Heights and maybe a strong defensive position in the Sinai, in face of Egypt, but all the rest should go back.

"There are almost a million Arabs on the West Bank. If we hold it, annex it, what kind of a state will Israel be, part-Jewish, part-Arab? No, that is not possible. Also, we are not colonialists, not imperialists. We must not rule over Arabs. Not on the West Bank, not in Gaza. On the other hand, the Arabs must agree to let Jews live in ancient Jewish settlements. Why should the Jews not live in Hebron, an historic Jewish city? Do the Christians and Arabs not live in Nazareth, in freedom under Israel? We should place tough conditions on freedom for Jews if we give back Arab lands.

"We favor the creation of a Palestinian state for the Arabs of Palestine, just as we have a Jewish state. But on condition that they don't use their territory to make war upon us. That is the main problem involved in return of territories, which is a major step towards peace. How to be sure that the Arabs won't use returned territories as a launching ramp for war—that is the question, the big question. I don't know the answer."

Yoel scratched his stomach, hitched up his trousers, frowned. An idea was gestating and troubling him.

"Frankly, we need a new 'cultural revolution,' something like the fervor of 1948. Our rich citizens should open their arms and purses for the immigrants and take a big load off the state budget, so that the state could do more for old immigrants, thus ending the rivalry and jealousy between the old immigrants, the Afro-Asians, living in bad conditions, and the new immigrants from Russia, who get good new accommodations."

We kept trying to steer this student leader to talk to us about student affairs.

"You want to know about our students. Well, the truth is they are not very idealistic. Partly it is our educational system, which teaches us that Israel is a great country, our leaders miracle-workers—as they are—and that we are right about everything. This tends to make us self-satisfied, even arrogant.

"Since we are a great country, why should we not have a great life for ourselves, make a lot of money, and so forth? Perhaps, too, the pendulum had to swing from our idealistic parents to a more pragmatic generation. Interested only in ourselves, I admit.

"You know, I organized a big public meeting between American students here and Israeli students. There are twelve thousand registered Israeli students at Tel Aviv University. Only four showed up for the meeting. The Americans were very disappointed and hurt.

"I went around and saw my fellow-students the next day to find out what had happened. They told me they all supported *aliya,* immigration, particularly of Americans, but they had too much to do—their studies, part-time jobs—and had no time for meetings. That's true, you know; a lot of the students have to work, and the school study schedules are heavy. It's hard to organize student activities here. And then the students are older, and don't care much about student activities. In truth, they are not students; they are men and women getting a degree."

Yoel frowned again; he was unhappy all through the interview, not with us, not with our questions, but with the answers that the truth obliged him to make.

"You know, there's a lot of bullshit along with the truth. I was a student, I worked part-time, I had a tough schedule, but I found time to concern myself with general activities. I'm only twenty-seven, so I'm part of the young generation, but I must say that those five years younger than myself are already different from me. I think the young generation, below twenty-five, looks like a selfish one, without social conscience. I don't like it, I fear it; it's not good for Israel. It's not very Jewish. They're a new kind of Israeli, these kids, a new kind of Jew. They worry me.

"They all worry me—the Ashkenazim, who don't care about anything but getting ahead for themselves, and the Black Panthers, who make me sick imitating the Black Power rebels in America. That makes no sense at all. The two extremes are bad: pragmatists without social concern and rebels without a true cause. Oh, sure, the Panthers and other disadvantaged Israelis have a real grievance, but a grievance is not a cause.

"What's the difference? Well, a grievance is tactical. I mean, things are not being done efficiently, so complain. Okay. But a cause is strategic; it grows out of a bad social policy, a bad philosophy. That's not the case in Israel. Our social philosophy is good, but not always carried out as well as possible. The Black Panthers don't make this distinction."

Yoel turned to his friend Michael Kleiner to ask what he thought. Michael is the grandson of the owner of the Rowal cafés of Tel Aviv, a rich leading family of Israel.

"I think we have talked ourselves into believing we are 'super-Jews,' " said Michael.

"In 1948, our parents created this state against all odds, against the whole world. Besides, Jews have played an extraordinary role in world history, well beyond our numbers. Moses, Jesus, Spinoza, Marx, Einstein, Freud—the greatest thinkers of history. Jews are rarely average; we are either very good or very bad, very idealistic or not at all. We are a unique people, a chosen people, chosen for exemplary fortune or misfortune. Maybe now, at last, we will become ordinary people. Is that good or bad? I really don't know."

Michael's intervention recalled to mind a story told us by Walter Eytan when he was Israeli Ambassador to Paris.

One day, his French driver asked him, "Your Excellency, how many of you are there in the world?"

"You mean Israelis?" asked Eytan.

"No, I mean Jews," said the Frenchman. "How many Jews are there?"

"Well, we do not have a precise census, but something around thirteen and a half million," Eytan replied.

"Ah," said the Frenchman. "Now, Monsieur l'Ambassadeur, can you tell me how many Chinese there are?"

"Oh, about seven hundred and fifty million."

*"C'est remarquable!* Seven hundred and fifty million Chinese and only thirteen and a half million Jews. How come I never meet any Chinese?"

It is true that one meets many Jews and few Chinese around the world. It is true that Jews have had an impact on world history and still have an impact on world affairs out of all proportion to the numbers of Jews in the world or the numbers of Israelis, one thousandth of the world's population. Sometimes the Jews change the world, as with Einstein. Sometimes they are the victims of a world shock, as in the tragic murder of the Israelis at the height of the XXth Olympiad in Munich in September, 1972.

One cannot truly say that the Jews chose their fate, their geniuses, their tragedies. Only the most religious can believe they were chosen. Whatever the truth, their fate has been and is out of all proportion to their numbers.

Would they willingly choose to lose their genius if it meant losing their tragedy?

To judge from the attitudes of the new Israelis, the new Jews of Israel, one is tempted to say yes. Young Israelis certainly do not seek an exemplary role in the world, even in Israel itself. If this tendency is confirmed by the years ahead, then we may be living on the threshold of a complete change in Jewish life and in the Jewish role in the world.

We want to emphasize the words "if" and "may be," for

it is too early in the evolution of the new generation to make definitive statements, but, as conscientious reporters, we feel it is legitimate to mention the existence of this new, startlingly different tendency.

That we found strong evidence of this tendency in the general population of the young is one thing; that it also evidenced itself so sharply among the college and university students, the élite, the future intellectual leaders, is even more persuasive.

We pursued this investigation further, to the élite of the élite, the medical, engineering, and scientific communities among the young generation, between twenty-five and thirty. We visited with them at Technion in Haifa, at the Medical Faculties of the Jerusalem Medical School, the Hadassah Hospital, and at the famous Weizmann Institute in Rehovoth, near Tel Aviv.

# V

# *The Scientific Israelis*

*Hast thou perceived the breadth of the earth? declare if thou knowest it all. . . . Where is the way where light dwelleth?*
—JOB 38:18–19.

T H E Weizmann Institute sprawls like an American campus, with a mix of easy informality, complex disciplines, and esoteric research equipment. It was headed in the summer of 1972 by a famous American medical researcher, Dr. Albert Sabin, discoverer of the Sabin vaccine for polio. The best young brains in Israel and some of the best brains in the world, among visiting researchers, are gathered together at the Weizmann Institute, Israel's microcosm of Harvard, Columbia, M.I.T., and Cal Tech, with that extra feeling of community and trailblazing one used to find in the early days at Los Alamos.

Yadin Dudai is thin, nervous, quick to smile or frown, with bright eyes, the in-curving fingers of an artist, the shoulder-hunch of a scholar who has spent long hours bending over books or test tubes.

He is a biophysicist, completing his doctorate at the Weizmann Institute. He hopes to do postdoctoral work at NASA, in the United States, on extraterrestrial biology.

His father is an insurance agent, who came to Israel as an illegal immigrant to Palestine, obtained residence papers, and then went to Poland to bring his wife back with him. Yadin's brother is a TV reporter, taking university extension courses, as is Yadin's wife.

"She is not seeking a career. She studies for pleasure, to have something to do during my long hours in the lab. Yes, I suppose, too, because she thinks it is proper for the wife of a scholar to be educated."

Yadin expressed surprise at our question about Women's Lib.

"Women's Lib? What for? My wife is free, free to do what she wants—within the limits of her responsibilities, of course. The children, the house, her studies. Well, I have limits on my freedom, too. Do I want to start a Men's Lib?

"My wife does not like to cook. She is a bad cook. You see how thin I am? Well, I don't complain. Eating is not so important. Besides, when I come home from the Institute very tired, I don't care to eat much at night. We just throw something together.

"No, men and women are not completely equal in everything. There are very real differences. You take my field, science; women are not as good at biology as men. Oh, I know, you'll tell me about great scientists like Marie Curie, Irène Curie. They are the exception that prove the rule.

"Some of the functions of the brain are influenced by hormones. Female hormones are different in intellectual effect from male hormones—for example, take long-range thinking. If you want a long-range program, you must function evenly, steadily. Well, a woman can't do that, because of her monthly changes. Because the biological background of a woman is changing, not stationary, it is not as suited to long-range projects as a man's. It is, indeed, harmful for long-range projects.

"There are sexual differences, racial differences, genetic differences among humans. You know that Jews do not come from the same biological background as other peoples, according to the latest findings of biological researchers?"

Yadin grinned at the consternation on our faces, our frowns of disagreement.

"You don't like to hear that? Well, of course, it is a shock to sociologists, political scientists, reporters, liberals—all those who believe all humans are essentially alike in basic make-up: that a Jew's blood is the same as all others, and so forth.

"But in biology one must make *tabula rasa* of all prejudices, good or bad—that is, of all prejudgments—and judge what the microscope tells us. And it tells us that there are differences. That does not mean that there should be political or social or legal differences of treatment. There everyone should be equal. But in science this is not true.

"Jews are a nation and a people mainly because of a common culture and religion, not because of genetics. But we must continue to study the genetic differences and the changes over the years and mixtures of strains, such as the extraordinary mixtures now in Israel.

"We Jews are bound together by common bonds of tradition, history—even stronger than religious ritual—but above all because we feel Jewish, feel the family relationship, share the common security needs of defense, and also, it is true, because the world tells us we are Jewish and different. Whether you really are different or not does not matter. If the rest of the world thinks and says you are different, then for all practical purposes you are different.

"Homosexuals are different, are they not? As a biologist, I tell you that homosexuality is pathological and should be treated as such. But I can understand that a sociologist or psychologist might say, well, no, it is not a disease, it is a divergence from the norm, and treatment should take it into account. Then there are those who say why should they be treated? Let them alone to live as they wish. Well, I am a scientist and I do not feel competent in those other fields. For me, it is a case of pathology.

"Drugs? I have very strong prejudices against the use of drugs. I am trying, as a scientist, to rid myself of my own prejudice to observe the drug question scientifically. I intend to start experimenting with hash, to find out what the reactions are, but for the moment I can't bring myself to do it.

"The drug problem is not yet a serious one in Israel, but it seems, according to the statistics, to be on the rise every year. Jews from the African countries brought the 'hash' habit with them. And now it is being brought in, and made chic, by Americans. That's not good. We ought to know more about it.

"Yes, I do think nicotine is, for the moment, a greater danger. Israelis smoke much too much. Maybe any smoke is too much. But I'm inclined to feel that only addictive drugs should be made illegal. Government should interfere as little as possible in what people do.

"Myself, I don't smoke or drink. I suspect that the drug problem may become worse if peace comes. The tensions of the threat of war are a natural stimulant; if they are removed, it is possible that youth may turn to unnatural stimulants.

"Has it been the reverse in America? Vietnam has increased the drug problem? Well, that may be a question of easy access for soldiers in Vietnam. Also of hatred for the war. If one is bitter, frustrated, one is more apt to turn to drugs. We young Israelis are not bitter or frustrated.

"I think you Americans were right to go into Vietnam and to stop the communist aggression. It is tragic you could not do it quickly. It has lasted too long with very bad effects on you and this is a great worry for us, because America is so important to us.

"America has been very helpful to Israel and it has not been easy, for you have many interests in the Arab countries and the power struggle with Russia. I admire America very much, although frankly I'm a little afraid of America, as everybody in a small country is afraid of a big volatile atomic power. But I hate Russian-Chinese systems more than anything and I hope America will never fail to stand up for freedom in the world.

"I'm not afraid of the Arabs. I think the present situation of no war-no peace is the best we can hope for. It keeps us united. In full peace, our individual differences would become greater, our emotions more passionate, and Israel would be in danger from within."

Yadin laughed, pushed his slide rule back and forth, as he did throughout our talk, and said, "But I think the Arabs will save us from ourselves. Every time there is a protest meeting or the signs of a split here, the Arabs do something terrible and bring us together."

He thought a long time before answering a question about his politics.* We found this hesitation in many interviews. It was not based on a reluctance to talk about politics but a difficulty in articulating political views. We found the young Israelis to be among the least politicized Jews we have met anywhere in the world.

"I am not committed politically or sociologically. If elections were held today, I would vote the government coalition because there is no other valid choice. Now, if Dayan would quit the coalition and form his own party again and go out to campaign on a new program—well, I would support him. So, I think, would most young voters.

"But at the moment there is no youth-oriented candidate, no youth party, no real youth movement. We grumble a lot about the *hazkenim*—the old ones—but do little to replace them."

Yadin laughed and asked us: "Did you see the cartoon by Dosh?

"Dosh said that the young generation in Israeli politics has no chance: 'Biology is against them—the old ones will out-live them.' "

Yadin said that in every election the youth vote split along the same lines as the adult vote, with little discernible difference in trends. "The Labor coalition will likely be in power a long time, with and after Golda."

On religion, Yadin evidenced the same indifference as on politics: "I am a High Holy Day Jew. I go to synagogue on Yom Kippur [the Day of Atonement]."

Yadin said he loved his army experience.

"I don't know why—after all, I am a scientist—but they gave me an assignment as a troop reporter, a journalist. Your profession."

He smiled slyly at us, the mocking smile we came to know

* For national opinion on this question, see Appendix: Continuing Survey, D2, p. 242.

so well as we met more and more young Israelis—not an un-friendly smile, but a kind of puckish, put-down attitude. "Yes, your profession. Marvelous fun! But not very scientific."

*     *     *

Avner Schoenfeld is twenty-seven, a biochemist at the Institute.

His parents are storybook copies of Israelis, for they came to Palestine fifty years ago, as ardent socialist Zionists, from Poland and Russia, the generation of Golda and Ben-Gurion.

"I, too, am a Zionist. I believe in the Jewish homeland for all Jews. But I am not religious, not even traditionalist. I am a cultural, an ethical Jew. I feel Jewish, therefore I am a Jew; that is enough for me. I hold no truck with all these arguments of the religious parties about who or what is a Jew. If you want to be Jewish, feel Jewish, you are a Jew.

"There is a difference between a Jew and an Israeli. A Jew in the Gola [the world outside Israel] can be a Jew but he is not an Israeli. Being an Israeli is a nationality. Being a Jew is a culture.

"I used to feel superior to the Gola Jew. I had a country, the Gola Jew had no country. It never occurred to me that an American Jew had a country of his own. It was stupid of me.

"When war came, I suddenly understood the importance to me of the Jew in America. We need our fellow-Jews, need their support, not just money but political. The Gola Jew is an indispensable force for Israel.

"I do not think there is any conflict between being a Jew and an American, or an American Jew for Israel. After all, America went to war twice in this century in Europe, to save the French and the British, to fight for democracy. Why should Americans therefore not be prepared to fight to defend the only truly democratic state in the Middle East, Israel?*

"No Jew should be embarrassed to support Israel, or tol-

---

* For national opinion on this question, see Appendix: Continuing Survey, C1, p. 239.

erate the charge he does so as a Jew. Israel is worthy of support by Jew and non-Jew, but above all by Jews. Why not?"

Avner is engaged to and will soon marry a twenty-three-year-old social worker.

"Of course my wife will work after marriage. First, she wants to, and she has the right to fulfill herself. Second, I want her to—I think she will be happier and our marriage will be better if she has her own interests. No, no, this has nothing to do with Women's Lib. I don't believe in movements of that kind. Let each individual decide what he or she wants to do.

"A movement for women alone is not a good idea. There should be strong movements for social justice for all sectors of the population. Making a movement just for women is a form of discrimination. Maybe it is needed in societies where women are really oppressed. Believe me, Jewish women are not oppressed."

Avner paused as a thought crossed his mind.

"Listen, religion is a bigger problem than women's rights. Religious fervor, the desire to impose religious rules on everyone—this can be a threat to the unity of a people. It is a potential threat here in Israel. Some say it is already a real threat. The religious groups already have special rights and privileges in the army."

Avner believes that immigration is very important for Israel. "They bring us new skills, new ideas."

He is very much opposed to the New Left. He votes for the Gahal—a right-wing party.

"The New Left is destructive. It is against everything and offers nothing. Communists, even fascists, have programs and sometimes can help a country, as in China. I don't like them, mind you, but I detest the New Left."

We heard Avner Schoenfeld's views expounded over and over again, among the élite intellectual groups, among workers, skilled and unskilled, among clerks, salesmen, every sector except the kibbutzim, where we found the most progressive, thoughtful, and compassionate group of young Israelis.

We do not quite trust our own samplings on politics, for they run counter to every voting pattern, every national poll. For what it is worth, however, and we think it is significant —we suspect that the national polls are behind current thinking—we found a strong movement to right of center and even to the far right among young Israelis. By far right, we mean that it is still within the democratic culture—there is no fascism or sign of it in Israel.

At least seven out of ten young people, even at university levels, indicated favorable views on Herut, Gahal, and other hard-line, rightist, nationalistic parties. Menahem Begin and Ezer Weizmann, and others who express tough views on peace, war, the occupied territories, are popular among the young.

The right has been held back by Dayan's refusal to join it. He is the most popular single personality in the country. He may hold the key to the future swing to right or left of center, depending on how he campaigns in the next elections.

\* \* \*

David Mirelman is thirty-one, but still qualifies in the outer limits of the Israeli youth sector. He was born in Argentina in 1941, came to Israel with his parents, as immigrants, in 1947, a year before the state was founded. He is, therefore, Israeli-bred, if not Israeli-born.

David is a microbiochemist at the Weizmann Institute.

The Mirelman family originally lived in Switzerland. David's father has a Ph.D. from Heidelberg University. David himself has received his Ph.D. from the Weizmann Institute. His mother is a high school graduate. His wife, a university graduate, teaches elementary school. They have two children and are planning to have one more. They live in the Ramat Gan suburb of Tel Aviv, a prosperous middle-class area, in a modern high-rise building.

The Mirelmans left Switzerland after the German-Austrian Anschluss, for fear that Hitler would eventually spread his domain all over Europe, including Switzerland. They went to Argentina. David still speaks fluent Spanish and part of this interview was conducted in Spanish by co-author Lucy Szekely. Robert Szekely conducted many interviews in Hungarian and Russian with the new immigrants.

"Our biggest governmental problem is opportunism. By that I mean there is not sufficient forward-planning. The government lives from crisis to crisis, dealing with problems when they grow critical. One day it is the Black Panthers, another day Arabs living in border villages; then it is housing, taxes, peace negotiations, the Rogers plan, Sisco arrives, Nahum Goldman wants to go to Cairo. Sufficient unto the day is the crisis thereof. That's no way to run a country.*

"Well, to be fair, it's not all the government's fault. We are a small country with big problems. It is hard to plan in the face of Arabs, Russians, and Americans, whose own policies whirl around the world, subject to drastic shifts. Nixon trading with the enemy, Russia—embracing Chou En-lai and Mao! Hard to look ahead and plan in such a world.

"I am not very committed politically but I would like to be able to vote for Dayan in the elections of 1973. Our system of voting for party lists, then the practice of coalition among parties, makes it difficult to vote for a man. I'm not even sure that Dayan would be good at the kind of political wheeling and dealing so necessary in Israeli politics. But maybe he could break or bend or otherwise alter the system. Anyway, he is a strong man; he knows how to deal with the Arabs, he understands their mentality.

"I think the answer to the Arab problem is to favor creation of a Palestinian state that would live in some kind of political-economic federation with us, or maybe a less formal kind

* For national opinion on this question, see Appendix: Continuing Survey, C5, pp. 240–241.

of trade arrangement. The Palestinians have got to have a homeland, find out what it is to run a country. It would absorb their energies, siphon off their passions, and we could look ahead then to a real peace.*

"We should not keep the Golan Heights—it is not our land by any standard. But the Arabs must not be permitted to remilitarize it and use it to shoot down upon our farmers in their fields.

"I would not want to keep the Sinai, but I would want to keep a bastion at Sharm-el-Sheikh and access to it, to defend our navigation through the Red Sea, the trade routes to Africa and Asia. They can strangle us there if we have no defense.

"The Americans want to keep the Russians out of the Indian Ocean, so they are not unhappy about the Suez Canal being closed. But it is not fair to us not to be able to use the Canal, then to tell us also to pull out of the Sinai. America wouldn't put up with it.

"Why, you have gone many thousands of miles to Vietnam to defend positions far less vital to you than the very positions we are being pressured to give up. Big powers are prone to tell us, 'Don't do as we do, do as we tell you to do.'

"Vietnam, to be blunt, was a stupidity. What if it does become communist? What is it to you that another ten million Asians become communist after seven hundred and fifty million Chinese and two hundred and fifty million Russians?

"Only Russia and America believe in monolithic communism. It's absurd. It offends the intelligence. And it is frightening to us, for a healthy, clear-thinking, friendly America is vital to Israel. We are all very distressed about Vietnam and hope it ends fast.

"I am most worried about the difficulties of life for our young people here in Israel. It is hard for a young couple to

* For national opinion on this question, see Appendix: Continuing Survey, A5, p. 235.

find an apartment, harder still to pay for it. We pay high taxes, on low wages.* But everything is given to the new immigrants, the *olim,* and to the settlers of new towns. Many of the immigrants think they are doing us a favor when they come, and they expect everything to be done for them. It is not fair to us who have been born and bred here, paid the taxes, fought the wars.* Zionism is a real problem. It causes severe social strains. Still, we have no choice, have we? We must do what has to be done."

* * *

Dafna Atlas is tall, dark-haired, olive-skinned, a stunningly handsome woman of twenty-eight, radiating health and intelligence. She is married to a physician. She is finishing her doctorate in biophysics at the Weizmann Institute. Her brother took his advanced degree in economics. Her father is an engineer, her mother a pediatrician. The Atlas family is well named. They seem to carry a world of knowledge on their strong backs.

Dafna's father was the first pilot of the Israeli Air Force and opened the first school for pilots. He was born and raised in Austria, came to Palestine in 1920, and married a Polish immigrant.

Dafna has one child, taken care of by a nurse while she works at the Institute. She plans to have four children.

"We have a number of women scientists at the Institute. I do not agree at all that women are unequal in any way to men in intellectual pursuits. Of course, we don't have as much muscle, but what difference does that make? As for our so-called monthly 'disturbances,' some women are disturbed, some are not. And I know a lot of men who don't have periods who are regularly disturbed. What nonsense!

"There are differences, may they never disappear. I confess I like a man to open a door for me, to show me cour-

* For national opinion on this question, see Appendix: Continuing Survey, D2, p. 242.

tesies, to be gallant. It's wonderful. That doesn't make me less of a biophysicist, does it?

"Perhaps men and women should have different roles, but can anyone argue that Golda hasn't been a strong leader? Has she been less of a Prime Minister than Eshkol before her?

"I want to research, not teach. Why should I teach because I am a woman? Some of my finest teachers have been men.

"No, I am not interested in politics. I voted in '68, but I will not vote next time. A waste of time. It's always the same bunch. The problems don't change and the solutions don't change. It's not so bad. Let them do it, I'll do my research.

"For relaxation, I like to play basketball. I'm on the national women's team. I love it. I get to travel from time to time for matches. My other favorite relaxation is to read. I love Hesse. My husband reads a lot, but only in French, so I read a lot of French books that he buys: Camus, Sartre, Malraux, Sagan.

"We Israelis, particularly the new generation, are not sporting enough—I mean do not practice enough sports. It's a Jewish mentality to train the mind, not the body. That's very bad, very bad. I am one of the few players on my team with advanced education. Most athletes are not highly educated. This, too, is bad. Athletes should be well educated; intellectuals should practice physical exercise.

"Listen, it is not easy to love one's husband, make a happy marriage, study for a doctorate, raise a child, and play basketball. But if I can do it, so can others. Our government does not have a good attitude towards physical training for all Israelis.

"I had a scholarship to study in Minnesota. I will tell you the truth—I did not like America. A beautiful country, but the people—well, I didn't really like them, I'm sorry to say.

"What bothered me? Well, they are superficial. They are very open, invite you to their homes, tell you their most intimate secrets, with no sense of privacy. Then you never see them again. They know someone for a day, and say 'Oh, that's a good friend.' I don't make friends in a day, but when I do it is for life. They are superficial.

"In Israel, if someone smiles at you and makes friendly overtures, you know it is because you have attracted them. But in America everybody smiles, everybody is friendly, and it doesn't mean a thing.

"Americans know nothing about Israel. They think we all go around on camels, praying all the time.

"And now, when they read what I say, they'll accuse me of being anti-American. I'm not anti-American. There are fantastic American achievements. I'm just telling you how I reacted as a human being to a different culture that I found not what I liked.

"I am not religious, nor traditionalist, and I care nothing about appearances or rituals. I celebrate Passover and major holidays as milestones of our great Jewish history.

"What do I think of marriage between Jews and non-Jews? Lama Lo! Why not! It is a person's right of choice.

"You know, now that I have told you what I think about Americans, maybe I'd better tell you what I think about Israelis. That surprises you? Well, I'll tell you, I don't like Israelis, either.

"Israelis are narrow-minded. They are square. They are selfish and arrogant. So am I, for that matter. I confess I don't care about politics, or social affairs, although I have to admit intellectually that it is a citizen's duty to care about vital questions of the state and society. Ours is a complex society. If highly educated people like myself turn our backs, that is dangerous. I admit it.

"There are, of course, many things I *do* like about my fellow-Israelis. We are very frank, outspoken. Visitors call it rude, but we do not mean to be rude. We are direct. We are not impolite but not particularly polite, either. We don't believe in manners. We sabras are naïve but also cynical. We are very provincial.

"These are personal opinions. I cannot claim to be a typical Israeli. After all, less than ten percent of the people have the higher education, income, and background of my family group. But I am not that atypical, either, in my views. Lots of young Israelis would agree with what I said about us, although we may disagree on the role of women and on other important questions of state."

\*   \*   \*

Yudith Sharon, age twenty-three, is in her third year of medicine. Her father is a doctor. The family came to Israel from Hungary in 1957, when she was nine years old.

"I guess my father will always be at least a little Hungarian. Once a Hungarian always a Hungarian. They say it's a profession.

"No, no, we won't exchange Hungarian jokes; we'll be at it all day.

"I'm an Israeli. No problem of identity.

"Zionism is the only hope of the Jews to survive in this world. They should all come here, but at least all Jews must understand that we are their ultimate hope and feel a full sense of responsibility for Israel.

"I vote for the government. We must have a solid majority. We can't afford the luxury of government and political crises. There is too much to do.

"Conservative? No, not exactly. Moderate, I'd say. Like most medical students. Who ever heard of a radical medical student? Our studies are too difficult for militancy. Besides, the study of medicine teaches us the value of the golden mean, of moderate ways, no excesses.

"America was right to try to stop the communists in Vietnam. It is tragic that you had to pay so terrible a price and were so unprepared for their kind of war in Asia, and didn't have a strong government as an ally. Israel is the right ally for the United States.

"We are not ritually religious down the line, but we believe that the kosher laws should be upheld. They are excellent, medically sound. I am opposed, however, to the official imposition of the Sabbath law. Let those who want to observe the Sabbath observe it but not impose it on the whole country. And there is nothing so infuriating as the segregation of women from men in the synagogue, and religious marriage and divorce laws. Antiquated and unfair.

"No, I am not a Women's Libber. There is no movement of this kind to speak of in Israel. I'm in medical school on equal terms with male students. I've no complaint."

\* \* \*

Zvi, in his second year of medicine, came from Rumania when he was twelve.

"Medicine absorbs all of my time, my thinking.

"I support the government. Golda is doing all right. She is a monument. We are proud of her.

"I am for Zionism because I know the world is anti-Israel, the world is anti-Semitic. Who can doubt it?

"America should give all aid to Israel; we are the only democratic nation in this part of the world.

"What a tragedy, Vietnam. You are right to fight communism, but it turned wrong and your people are against it, so the war should end, for it is tearing America apart.

"I want a chance to live in peace, want a wife and five children. My wife must raise the family. She can work if she wants to, but not as a career. A doctor's wife—that is a career in itself."

\* \* \*

Neri, twenty-five, is interning at the Hadassah Hospital. His parents are both university graduates who immigrated to Israel from Rumania in 1949 when Neri was three.

"I'd never be in medical school in Rumania, certainly not an élite school like this one. Thank God for Zionism, for Israel.

"I admire Dayan, vote for the Rafi Party, would like to see Dayan Prime Minister, but probably the central Labor Party will cling to power. All right, they're not so bad, just as long as Dayan sticks with them.

"I'm worried about an increase in drugs. Many of my friends, even medical students, are smoking 'hash.' All drugs should be outlawed.

"We all want to get married and have three, four, five kids. It's up to the women to raise the family.

"What? Should a woman doctor's husband stay home and raise the kids for her? That's very funny. I never thought of that. Well, I'll be damned!"

# V I

*The Kibbutz Is Dead!*
*Long Live*
*the Kibbutz!*

> *One generation passeth away, and another*
> *generation cometh: but the earth abideth for*
> *ever. . . . The thing that hath been, it is that*
> *which shall be; and that which is done is that*
> *which shall be done: and there is no new*
> *thing under the sun.*
>
> —ECCLESIASTES 1:4, 9.

As she walked through the Officers Club—tall, slim, with flowing blond hair falling over high Slavic cheekbones, wearing a smart tailored uniform, severely straight, except where she herself curved out of it—she seemed the perfect illustration of a Nordic beauty. Her name is Hadassa Bankir. She is an Israeli Jewish girl, twenty-three, an officer in the Israeli Army, a graduate of Hebrew University in Jerusalem, with degrees in Hebrew literature and philosophy. She was born in a kibbutz near Haifa, in northwest Israel. Her father emigrated to Palestine from Poland in 1928; her mother from Russia in 1932.

"I was born in 1948, the year we fought off the Arab invaders, the year Israel was born. I have a country of my own, unlike my parents. Israel, then, means more to me than being a Jew.

"This shocks you? It should not. It does not mean that I rate Jewishness less. It means simply that I accept the fact that I am a Jew, as my parents were. I was born Jewish. I do not marvel at this. What is marvelous is that I was born an Israeli, in a Jewish state—not a Pole like my father, not a Russian like my mother. Is this not marvelous?

"The kibbutz? I was happy there as a child. Life is free in a kibbutz. Never have I known such freedom, such security, such communion with others. My father is an agronomist. He also helped out by teaching biology and chemistry. We had a good life on the kibbutz. But my parents became disillusioned with kibbutz life when the kibbutz began to lose its original idealism, its socialism, its dedication, and became a more efficient, economic producing unit.

"My father said, 'If the purpose is to make money and to increase production, then why live in a socialist society which is not really socialist? I can do better on my own, have my own property, do what I like, instead of sharing everything and having my life regulated by the committee.'

"The kibbutz, for me, meant something different than it did for my father. I was born and raised there, so I did not question it, nor did I see what my father saw about its change from idealistic socialism to economic pragmatism. When I was taken from it, in 1956, I was only eight years old.

"What I realized later, outside the kibbutz, in normal society, demonstrated to me the weaknesses and strengths of the kibbutz. It makes for a very strong, secure, totally integrated communal society. But by the same token it fails to develop individual initiative. It does not prepare one for life in society. Kibbutzniks who leave have a difficult time in society except for one institution, the army, which is a communal society. That is why we kibbutzniks make such excellent soldiers and officers, why we have fought so well, have had so many more casualties proportionate to our numbers than any other segment of the people.

"Kibbutzniks are always at one with the group, work together, ready to sacrifice self for the group, feeling fulfilled and happy within the group. But we are often lonely and sad, because we have no very special friends. In the kibbutz, one does not choose one's friends; one is thrown together with everyone. That lends security and strength, of course, but humans yearn for special love, special friendship, for choice. At least, I do. I respect the kibbutz. I am glad I lived some formative years there. But I think it is a dream, a fairy tale. Very few Israelis of my age want to live in a kibbutz. Immigrant Jews do find security there. The kibbutz will endure, as dreams endure, but it is not Israel."

Hadassa smiled gently at us and said she hoped we were not disappointed in her lack of idealism. "Americans expect us all to be idealists. The people of the Holy Land." She laughed. "Holy Land? That is not a Jewish concept. Listen, let me tell you about the history of our homeland. Golda's generation made the revolution. My father's completed it. My generation wants to live. We want to be normal."

"We want to be normal."

We heard this phrase, in nearly identical words, in almost every one of two hundred interviews. We soon came to understand that by "normal" they meant they wanted to live in peace. But young Israelis rarely put it directly in terms of peace. We had to rephrase the question in different ways and often just ask directly, "Do you mean you yearn for peace?" before they would admit it.

Not that they are ashamed to admit that they are weary of the defense burden. When pressed, they would concede that the burden is very heavy. Every citizen is liable for military duty, some two years of active duty for women and three years for men, plus forty to sixty days a year on reserve call-ups, up to the age of fifty-five, with very few exemptions (certain orthodox sects, Arabs, severe physical handicaps, a widowed mother's need of a son).

General Shlomo Lahat, Chief of Army Manpower (who has, since this interview, retired), an Israeli hero for his exploits as a commander in the Sinai campaign, told us that Israel may be the only country in the world where young men, called up for military service, lie, cheat, go to family doctors for help in order to cover up any physical defect that might keep them out of the army.

"We have learned that our young people consider it a disgrace and a stigma for life not to have served in the defense of our country. We now try to take almost everyone, even the severely handicapped. After all, a boy with one arm can do office filing work. Among those with very poor eyesight there are fine brains. We need them all and they all have a right to participate. None wants to go through life saying the army rejected me. Consequently, our induction rate on draftees is over ninety-four percent of all called, by far the highest in the world."

General Lahat, better known in Israel by his nickname, "Tcheetch" (a shrill cry he screeched as anchor man on his tug-of-war team as a boy), confirmed what Hadassa Bankir had told us about the boys and girls who enter the army from the kibbutz.

"They have been born and raised in a collective society and take to army life like ducks to water. They know about teamwork and understand better than anyone the slogan 'All for one and one for all.' The kibbutz is now a very small part of Israeli society but a vital one. I hope it never disappears."

* * *

Israel's leading authority on the kibbutz movement, sociologist Dr. Haim Darin-Drabkin, chairman of the socialist intellectual review *New Outlook* and consultant to the United Nations, believes the kibbutz movement will not disappear but is undergoing and will yet undergo great change with important consequences for Israel and for other countries, many of which, particularly in the new nations of the world, have already been influenced by the Israeli model.

"It is true that some young kibbutzniks, like your Hadassa Bankir, do leave the kibbutz, either because their parents take them out or because they are confused or disillusioned by the dynamic changes taking place.

"The population of the kibbutzim is now only about 3.5 percent of the total population of Israel—very small, to be sure. But it has held steady at that figure for roughly a decade and seems likely to remain permanently at that level. The net population remains almost steady, with new immigrants joining the kibbutz to replace those who leave."

Dr. Darin-Drabkin found it particularly interesting that the kibbutz has attracted many young American immigrants to Israel. Young Americans, disillusioned with the materialism of American life and also disillusioned with the excesses and anarchy of the American youth movement, find a new communal idealism in the Israeli kibbutz. The same holds true

for young immigrants from communist countries, disillusioned with the "betrayal of socialism," the lack of freedom
or respect for the individual in Eastern Europe. Thus, young
men and women from the capitalist West and the communist
East find a new ideal in the Israel kibbutz.

Not that the kibbutz is without its own contradictions and
disillusions, as we heard from Hadassa and many other former kibbutzniks. The dilemma of the kibbutz had been
brought to a crisis peak by the constant imperatives of war
and national defense.

In the Six-Day War, soldiers recruited from the kibbutzim
accounted for some 25% of the casualties, although the
kibbutzim, as already noted, represent only about 3.5%
of the population. Their spirit of volunteering, their high
technical training and educational level, and their understanding of group action inevitably made them unit commanders of front-line troops.

"However," said Dr. Darin-Drabkin, "their sense of ful-
filling a national duty, growing out of their kibbutz idealism,
clashed with another high ideal of the kibbutz—humanitar-
ianism and its aim of providing a better future for all peoples.
The kibbutznik hates war, hates killing, although he is the
best of all soldiers.

"Everyone should read the extraordinary book *The Seventh Day*. It is a collection of transcripts of interviews conducted by a team of young Israelis asking soldiers what they
thought of the great victory in the Six-Day War. Well, on
that seventh day, right after the war, they did not speak as
conquering heroes.

"Our boys and girls spoke of their revulsion against the
blood and the killing, of the futility of war, of the need for
peace, for a political settlement. War may prevent a catastrophe. We cannot let ourselves be slaughtered and driven
into the sea. But war itself is a catastrophe and does not bring
solutions to the problems which caused it in the first place.

This is what our young people said.

"This is the strength and the future of Israel, to have young people such as we have, who do their duty but see clearly that it is not enough. And that, to a great degree, is the gift of the kibbutzim to our society.

"It is a tragedy that our young kibbutzniks, and many other young Israelis, are sure of themselves in only one direction: war. Yet they also know that it is a false direction. Israel was founded by humanitarian socialists who dreamed of a model state of social justice, shared labors, people living in peace, fighting only hunger, disease, and ignorance. That we should then find our ultimate expressions, our self-assurance, in war,* to kill or to be killed—that is the tragedy of Israel."

\* \* \*

The sense of serious malaise among the young generation of the kibbutzim became critical in the year following the Six-Day War as it gradually became apparent that the sacrifices of lives in the war may have saved Israel but brought no promise of peace or the end of killing. This malaise found strong expression in June of 1968 at the kibbutz of Ein-Shemer, one of the most prosperous and successful of the kibbutzim.

Ein-Shemer was to celebrate the fortieth anniversary of its founding, and the elders were planning a joyous celebration. But the young members of the kibbutz told them it was no time to celebrate, since they were still steeped in mourning for their comrades who had fallen in the war a year before. Instead, they said they preferred to hold a symposium, a frank and full public discussion of current trends both within and outside the kibbutz, and to give expression to the doubts which had been forming in their minds and hearts with the passing of time. Only by a real effort to find out what was

---

\* For national opinion on this question, see Appendix: Continuing Survey, D2, p. 242.

wrong and to correct it could they truly honor their dead and give full meaning to their sacrifice.

The symposium was held for four days and nights.

Each kibbutznik arose at the meeting and gave voice to his feelings and thoughts. Secretaries recorded all the statements and discussions and then transcribed them. These records, known as "The Dialogue of Ein-Shemer," provide one of the most poignant and instructive documents on the mood and mind of the new generation of Israel, of particular interest because they record the voices of the élite of the new generation, the most idealistic, the most motivated children of the utopian socialist dreamers who founded the nation.

Here are extracts taken from the records of the Dialogue:

"In the beginning the kibbutz was small, life was simple. Everyone knew his role and everyone was a participant. There was no hierarchy. Then the kibbutz grew and prospered and became a more complex social unity. Young sons became young men, not children, and thus, inevitably, there developed new and sometimes strained relationships between fathers and sons, between founders and followers.

"The rift deepens with each passing year. Modernization and mechanization have brought changes and breaks in the work cycle, and this has resulted in new attitudes, new social differentiations. Now instead of everyone being a participant, in full part, we perceive the emergence of 'providers' and 'dependents.' We see the rise of relativism, a small group of people who are active within the kibbutz and who hold the decisive levers of control over its affairs.

"The complexity of life creates a natural selection of leadership and hierarchy. Thus one begins to perceive political divisions and categories, 'the rulers' and 'the ruled.' This leads to attitudes of 'insiders' and 'outsiders.' Estrangement takes root. The feeling of mutuality, of communality weakens. If this evolution is not halted and new directions found, then it is the end for the original ideal of the kibbutz.

". . . I claim that the kibbutz, as it stands today, cannot continue to exist. The kibbutz was created as an instrument for achieving two purposes: national objectives of agricultural sufficiency and defense of frontier territories; and the humanitarian aim of creating a new man. If in the first aim it succeeded—as it undoubtedly did—in the second it set itself a goal which it was unable to achieve in the short span of time that we have had, assuming that the creation of a new man is at all possible of achievement.

"The inner conflict, in my opinion, stems from the fact that the kibbutz set itself standards which aimed at perfection. From an ethical point of view, it was believed that a member of the kibbutz had to be perfect or as near as possible to perfection. From the social point of view, we were all expected always to live in harmony with all others. Our cultural values naturally were to be of the highest. But the moment one sets oneself such a goal of perfection, any deviation by any member who cannot attain or maintain such perfect standards of the ideal creates divisions and internal dissensions which weaken the group.

"The founders of the kibbutz, and we, too, the young members, are guilty of a large measure of arrogance. The belief that planned upbringing can change human nature itself, change man's emotional and spiritual make-up, this is to look down from Olympus."

"We are the 'next generation' and we are asked to carry on in someone else's footsteps. That is duller, more difficult, not physically but emotionally. 'To carry on,' that is a mundane motivation compared with the ideal 'I am going to build something myself.' Generations change . . . we were born different from those who founded our kibbutz, different in the way we feel, different in our way of thinking and acting and reacting. And the question for us is whether we shall be able to create something not only for the economy of the kibbutz but in making the kibbutz a part of ourselves, our own achievement, our own fulfillment."

"The kibbutz of yesterday had to solve the problem of want, of need—physical need and the spiritual need to create a community. Today the kibbutz must address itself to a new need: a way of life. It must enable its members to develop to their fullest, to develop their own personalities, so they can feel complete, so they can overcome the phenomenon—lack of communication—which is so widespread throughout the modern world and which makes all men strangers."

"Today, our aim—the aim of the young generation—is to build upon the base laid down by the founding generation a new society where each individual feels self-fulfillment, the fullest development of his personality, a society where people are not sacrificed upon an altar. Not 'The Kibbutz,' and the people who live for it, but a community of the kibbutz, in small letters, not capitals, a kibbutz which is the sum total of its individuals, a community whose purpose is the people who live in it."

One of the most perceptive of the observations in the symposium came from a member in his middle thirties, old enough to remember the early days and the original inspirations and to appreciate what the founders had done, but young enough to understand why the new generation was demanding change.

"I see the kibbutz as a unique creation, formed out of difficult conditions on the one hand and socialist dreams on the other. It was felt that the Garden of Eden was being recreated. Hopes were high; it was possible to change everything at once: the nation, world, man. That is how they set out, how they tried to build a life where they would change the patterns formed by generations.

"Where previously there had been private property, now it would belong to all. Instead of material reward, there would be spiritual reward. Upbringing and education would begin to change the behavior and then the nature of man. The community would raise the children, not the mother. A new culture would be created . . . why, they would change God himself.

"It seems to me that this mistaken conception, that mankind could be changed, indeed overnight, and that society can be based upon ideological motivation, is the cause of recurring internal conflict in the kibbutz system. It has caused a chasm, of which we are all aware, between ordinary people and lofty ideals. And this gap is most acutely felt in the second generation.

"The system—born of historic necessity—made man an instrument, grist for the mill of society. It was a system in a desperate hurry, wanting to achieve all its aims at once, wanting the entire chain to be forged, without realizing that the strength of the chain is the strength of each of its links, the wealth, happiness, and human relations of its members, which is the only true expression of the strength of the community.

"Today we all yearn for a higher stage—higher because it is more humanistic: that kibbutz life shall not clash with personal fulfillment. We want to be a chain in the best sense of the word; that is, with each link complete in itself and the chain itself solid. The kibbutz must be the link force, the sum total of the human and national aspirations of the individual links. We want to be part of the nation, part of the building process, but not at the cost of being untrue to ourselves. In the final count, man has no significance except as part of society, but society has no significance without men. Only when man is the prime purpose, the true end, can he also serve as a means.

". . . Ideology, which was the lifeblood of the kibbutz,

has no place in the new reality. . . . The kibbutz must create a new philosophy to replace the old ideology. Even as it is now, it will continue to exist, but with ever greater strains. With a new philosophy, a new reality moving toward a synthesis of societal and individual needs, it will evolve on healthier foundations. No society can exist for long without a spiritual foundation, and particularly is this true of a society as unique as the kibbutz."

This symposium of 1968 and many similar discussions we heard among the kibbutzim in the summer of 1972 confirm not only the existence of a deep-rooted malaise but, more importantly, confirm the deep-rooted health of the kibbutzniks.

The young generation, brought up and educated in the kibbutz, known mainly for its technical skills on the farms and its courage on the battlefields, has shown and is showing the quality of its intellectual perceptions and intellectual courage.

It was not easy for young men and women to stand at a public meeting with elders they revered and deliver themselves of searching, even wounding criticism. They managed to do this without ever being offensive, insulting, or abrasive. There was no note of self-pity or of despair or outrage. This was not and is not a "youth rebellion," such as the movements which shook America and France in the spring and summer of 1968.

The dialogues revealed a wide generation gap, but it was truly a gap, something bridgeable, and not a front line between hostile forces arrayed in violent opposition. The nature of the criticism and of its expression does honor to a movement which knew how to bring up a generation able to speak its mind, straight, clear, sometimes passionate, but never in anger, never escapist, never destructive.

The kibbutzniks have come to understand that a community, a committee, is not a substitute for a mother and a father—at the very moment when Western intellectual left movements contemptuously disparage "the nuclear family." But they do not dismiss the past as a great mistake of the old founders.

If the community cannot satisfy human needs by acting *in loco parentis,* young Israelis also know that mother and father are no complete substitute for the community. They seek a new synthesis of communal and individual needs, not a swing of the pendulum from one to the other. This is what they mean by "the new reality."

Gideon Samet, thirty-year-old editor of *Ha'aretz,* a very young age for so important a post in a gerontocracy such as Israel, who admires the achievements of the kibbutzim while wanting no part of kibbutz life for himself, constantly uses the very same phrase that runs throughout the kibbutz dialogues: "the new reality."

We will meet Samet at greater length later—he is an exceptionally articulate, lucid thinker and speaker, a leading light among the new generation of the first Israelis. At this point, one thought of his is pertinent to the crisis of the kibbutz, a crisis far more than important to Israel's future, and to the future of those in the world who seek, as the kibbutz members do, to find the right balance between generations and between society and the individual.

"Our parents and grandparents, those slightly mad pioneers, the giants who cleared the ground and built this nation, performed their majestic feats partly out of sheer necessity—there was nothing but desert and swamp; they had to clear it and build—and partly—mainly, I guess—propulsed forward by the sheer force of their dreams and their faith.

"They never stopped to say, 'Should we clear a potato patch here, or plant cotton there, or raise sheep over there?' Or, 'Is alfalfa more important than cotton, or cotton more important than sheep? Perhaps a bicycle factory is needed first, or should housing come before or after planting?'

"No, our founders said with breathtaking simplicity: 'Let

there be a potato patch, a cotton field, a flock of sheep, bicycles, factories, and housing. Anywhere, everywhere, and right away.'

"It is not for us, the new generation, to say that our forefathers were right or wrong. How can we possibly recreate for our own consiousness the circumstances under which they had to operate? It is for us to say to them, 'May God bless you. We thank you, we love you for what you did, for this Jewish state you created for us, where we live in freedom in our faith.'

"But, that being said, we have a right to say something now for ourselves and for the kind of state we want to live in and in which we want to bring up our own children, to give them something as great as our parents gave us.

"Bruno Bettelheim wrote a wonderful book, called *Children of the Dream*. That is what he called us. True enough, but not completely true. Our parents realized the dream; in that sense, we are its children. But we are much more than that. We have to live not in the hopes of a dream, as our parents did, but with the reality that follows its attainment. In that sense, we are the children of reality.

"We do not say, 'Let there be a potato patch, and scratch it into the nearest soil.' We must say, 'Should there be a potato patch? And, if so, where is the best place to put it? How big should it be and what kind of potatoes should be planted? How much irrigation will it need; how many and what kind of pesticides, and how will that affect our environment? Or do we need more cotton, more tools, or is there a more nutrient, efficient food than potatoes?'

"This, in fact, is the new reality, otherwise known as pragmatism and efficiency.

"Not very glamorous, eh?

"Doesn't quite compare with Moses leading our people out of the wilderness, or Ben-Gurion draining the malarial swamps while editing a newspaper and reviving and modernizing the Hebrew language and protecting the fields from Arab bandits and arms supplies from British police?

"Nothing like Golda leaving Russia, becoming a school-teacher in Milwaukee, rallying the World Zionist Movement, sailing through naval patrols to land on the beaches of Palestine in a leaky tub called the *Pocahontas,* rising through the ranks to become Prime Minister in her mid-seventies, carving out for herself a niche as one of the greatest women and greatest leaders in history?

"No, we are nothing like that and never will be, for the imperatives of today and tomorrow do not call for such heroic, epic deeds. This is not an age of heroes. Our reality is not so brilliant, so colorful as the dream. But it is not without its importance, you know. Not without its challenge."

# VII

## What Price Peace?

> *And he shall judge among many people,*
> *and rebuke strong nations afar off; and they*
> *shall beat their swords into plowshares and*
> *their spears into pruninghooks: nation shall*
> *not lift up a sword against nation, neither*
> *shall they learn war any more.*
>
> *—MICAH 4:3.*

LIPSKI'S Restaurant, atop the rise in Jaffa, is a small oasis of excellent, if limited, cuisine in the desert of Israeli restaurants. With only seven or eight tables, Lipski can give full attention to the cooking and service required for so few guests. His specialty, much appreciated by the irreverent high society of Tel Aviv, is roast pork, which he gets from pigs raised for him by a Christian farmer.

One of the main attractions at Lipski's is a handsome young couple who live across the street and often drop by for a drink, cigarettes, or dinner: Harona and Assaf Dayan.

Harona, a television producer, and Assaf, an actor, are slender, supple, graceful, and in their mid-twenties. They look like their counterparts in the New York television and movie world who congregate at P. J. Clarke's or Elaine's.

Born and raised in Israel, they look nothing like, and are nothing like, the stereotypical world image of the sabra, the muscular, sun-browned pioneer, hoe in hand, gun slung on shoulder. Indeed, even in the kibbutz and in the Nahal military-agricultural settlements, few young Israelis look anything like the legendary sabra. Although technically any Israeli born in Israel is a sabra—the word simply means a native-born fruit, prickly outside, sweet and soft inside—the time of the sabra, the soldier-farmer, was really the era of Moshe Dayan, not of Assaf.

Assaf spoke frankly about his father and the difference between the generations when we left Lipski's to have a nightcap with him in his penthouse (which his father bought) in a de-luxe "high-rise" (eight stories is a high-rise in Jaffa) overlooking the Mediterranean.

"To a great extent, the army, the defense Establishment, they determine—well, influence greatly—our political policies. Moshe Dayan is not only a folk hero, he is a semi-divinity, except, of course—" Assaf grinned—"we Jews worship only one God.

"I do not approve of some of those policies, particularly on the occupied—excuse me, the 'administered territories,' to use the official euphemism. I hold opposition views on relations with the Arabs, on peace negotiations. Ever since we were born—my generation, the state—there has been war—three major wars—guerrilla fighting, a state of siege. This is no way to live. There must be another way. There must be an end to this. If there is a high price for peace, then let's find out what it is and see whether the price is right.

"Now, please, don't write, as so many journalists have, that Dayan's son is a dove, that he is in conflict with his father, that young Israelis want peace at almost any price. That would be such a deformation of the truth that it would be a lie.

"The truth is rarely simple. But I will try to make it clear.

"I admire my father and his generation. I trust him, trust him more than anyone else on most issues. He is wise and he is brave. So don't put me into rebellion against him. I am not. But I have my own views on the territories, on the Arabs, on the central issue of peace. On this, I oppose the government's hard line, or, more exactly, ambiguous, unclear policies. This doesn't make me a dove or my father a hawk.* He is part, an important part, of a government with which I disagree on important issues but support on many others. No more, no less.

"I think you will find this true of the majority of young Israelis, except for small minorities. The right-wing youth wants to keep all the territories and consolidate them into a Greater Israel. Left wingers want to give up everything in advance of any negotiations. Most of us are not that extreme, not that naïve."

* For national opinion on this question, see Appendix: Continuing Survey, A2, p. 234.

Sammy Davis, Jr., entered the room via the hi-fi set and celebrated the joys of a day like today as the doorbell rang and friends came in to visit. Scotch was poured and clouds of cigarette smoke swirled around African masks and sculptures. Very much like a New York evening, with the exception of the cigarette smoke.

Many young Americans are off nicotine; if they smoke, it is more often pot. But young Israelis are chain-smokers, nicotine and pot both, in penthouses in Tel Aviv and Jaffa and on the kibbutzim. Accurate statistics are hard to find, but, judging from wide experience, we would guess that Israelis are the smokingest people in the world. Smoke may well be a greater menace than the Arabs.

Neither Assaf nor Harona nor their friends and fellows ever made it clear to us just what their policy was to advance the advent of peace, or to settle the question of the occupied or administered territories. On some specific issues, however, there was clarity and virtual unanimity: Jerusalem is the capital of Israel, the very heart of Jewish history, culture, and faith. Jerusalem must not again be divided or put under any kind of international administration.

Israelis put no faith whatsoever in the United Nations.* The large number of Afro-Asian-communist bloc votes, the selfish cynical interests of the Security Council permanent members—the Great Powers—are well known to Israelis, who expect no favor from that quarter.

Israelis have not forgotten U Thant's immediate acquiescence to Nasser's demand to remove U.N. border-security troops from the Suez and the Sinai, clearing the way for an Egyptian invasion of Israel, a major factor in setting off the Six-Day War.

"Teddy" Kollek, Mayor of Jerusalem, speaks for most Israelis when he states the case of Jerusalem:

* For national opinion on this question see Appendix: Continuing Survey, A5, p. 235.

"Do they want to divide it, or administer it, for the betterment of its citizens, for freedom of worship and movement and speech? No, of course not! Jerusalem was not free under the Jordanians. Jews were not permitted to enter the Jordanian sector, to worship at their most revered shrine: the West Wall, the Wall of Lamentations.

"In Jerusalem, united capital of Israel, everyone is free to worship or not to worship as each sees fit. Christian pilgrims crowd the Via Dolorosa. Moslems come at will to the Mosque of Omar. They thrive, they prosper, they are free. What more do they want, what rights does the world seek that do not already exist in the City of David?

"Christians do not complain about the Israelization of Nazareth, a sacred Christian shrine. They do not demand that the location of the Grotto of Mary would justify an international administration over Nazareth. What makes Jerusalem so special that it be submitted to a special regime? Since when does the existence of religious shrines play a decisive role in the determination of political sovereignty over a city?

"Any Israeli, any Jew in the world can give the answer to that readily: since the Jews took over Jerusalem. Every Israeli is convinced that the world cares little about his fate. Most Jews would agree that the world cares little about Jews."

Almost every Israeli, in all age groups and classes, is agreed that Jerusalem will never be divided or abandoned. The world may protest, the U.N. may resolve, but Israelis pay no attention. They go on building their capital, extending its residential sectors, consolidating their defenses and communications, increasing the income, health, and progress of its citizens, making plans to wipe out the festering Musrara slums, breeding ground of dangerous social diseases, origin of the Black Panther movement (more about that phenomenon later).

The old barriers have been torn down between "East" and "West" Jerusalem. Some rubble and the skeletons of houses can still be seen, but they are almost gone and will soon be only a memory. Tens of thousands of Arabs live, and many more work and visit, in Israeli Jerusalem with a minimum of conflict and crime. As Joseph, the guide, correctly asserted, Jerusalem is a far safer, cleaner, healthier city than New York, Chicago, or almost any American big city of a half-million and more residents.

For the first few years after its liberation in 1967, there was tension in Jerusalem, fear of terrorism. By the summer of 1972, the tensions seemed all to have been dissipated. Israelis were even beginning to joke about Jerusalem, a sure sign of confidence.

One story current in 1972 told about Uncle Shlomo, a recent immigrant from New York who had spent his life dreaming of going to Israel.

"Open the gates of Israel!" he would shout at protest meetings in United Nations Plaza. His great day came, and he arrived in Israel, and then, to their astonishment, his nephews found him running around the Knesset in Jerusalem shouting, "Open the gates of Israel!"

His nephews surrounded him, tried to quiet him.

"Uncle Shlomo, please stop shouting. You are in Israel, in your beloved city of Jerusalem."

"I know, I know, but I want to get out!"

The joke is based upon an element of truth. Some immigrants discovered that Israel is not a land of milk and honey, that life is hard, work hours long, prices high, and taxes so crushing as to be almost confiscatory. At one time, in the fifties, almost as many people were leaving Israel as coming in. But today, and for the past decade, net immigration (those leaving deducted from those coming in) is overwhelmingly positive in total.

Another story, very revelatory of a certain Jewish mentality, particularly among those over sixty, tells of a family patriarch presiding over the Sabbath dinner and concluding it, every Friday night for fifty years, with the traditional Jewish toast: "Next year in Jerusalem!"

The entire family joyously celebrated the victory in the Six-Day War and the liberation of all Jerusalem. Yet the very next Sabbath night, the old man once again raised his glass, his eyes flashing upward as though to warn God that his patience would not be eternal, and shouted, "Next year in Jerusalem!" His children, astonished, remonstrated, "But, Papa, we won the war. You know that Jerusalem is ours now."

The old man glared at the family, beat his breast, and roared, "What are you trying to do, kill my hopes?"

Most Jews, particularly those in the Diaspora, less so the Israeli Jews, have been living with dreams and hopes for so long that they feel lost without them, find it difficult to adjust to a new reality, the hard reality of what follows the attainment of a dream.

The long years of fighting to attain a Jewish state were the years of courtship; the creation of the state and its early years were the honeymoon days. Now Israelis have to face a long life together, with all the adjustments that must be made for a successful marriage. Inevitably there are quarrels, conflicts, even desertions and divorces between citizens and the state, as between man and woman.

These family conflicts emerge quickly once the subject is changed from the status of Jerusalem to the other territories and the hopes for peace.

The government claims that it has taken no definitive position on future frontiers but that everything—except Jerusalem—can be and will be discussed once the Arab nations consent to direct negotiations on the basis of recognizing Israel's right to exist behind recognized and secure frontiers. Beyond this general statement, the government of Israel says very little that is not ambiguous and subject to varying interpretations.*

* See pp. 136–137 for the Prime Minister's statement of policy.

The majority of the country and the majority of the young citizens from eighteen to twenty-nine, the ones who have to bear the brunt of the defense and the fighting when it breaks out, support the government's prudent position.

"Peace is worth more than scrub desert, of course. We want peace, not territory. But we must be sure the territories will not be used as a base to attack us." That is the general majority sentiment.

There is, however, a growing significant minority view which argues that a golden opportunity was lost immediately after the Six-Day War when a generous, imaginative initiative might have won the peace for which all yearn.

A professor in Tel Aviv University Law School told us that he and many of his students believe risks must be taken for peace and that a supposedly "prudent policy" was, in fact, not prudent but fearful and could, in the long run, lead to more war.

"The Jewish birth rate is under four percent; the Arab birth rate, both inside Israel and in the neighboring countries, is over four percent. We are even now less than three million Jews, with a half-million Arabs inside our gates and more than eighty million surrounding us.

"In a strange way, Arab governments have been our best allies by their failure to advance the progress of their people, to educate them and rally them soundly rather than hysterically to a true cause and a close identification with their societies. But we cannot count on this being so forever. Now, when we are strong and confident and victorious, however heavily outnumbered, is the time for us to make the supreme effort to find the price of peace. Later it may be too late."

The professor's is a minority voice in public, but it does not take too long a sojourn in Israel to begin to sense that his is also the brooding fear, rarely expressed but felt even by the majority.

Among the most critical minority voices are those of the

Siah (New Left) movement, a small but vocal group of intellectuals. We spoke with a number of them at Tel Aviv University, at Haifa, and at Hebrew University in Jerusalem:

"We are not starry-eyed dreamers. We know very well that the territories we occupy were used as springboards of invasion and threaten our survival. From the Golan Heights, Syrian artillery could, and did, fire down into our farmlands as easily as shooting goldfish in a bowl. Some of us lived in the kibbutzim on the Lake of Kinneret [Galilee] and had to build an iron curtain in front of our refectory windows because Jordanian snipers were shooting into the dining room when we gathered for meals.

"We know that the Gaza Strip is a dagger poised at the heart of Tel Aviv and that we could not survive if a powerful Egyptian Air Force were based there, within minutes of our homes. Had we not destroyed Nasser's air fleet on the ground at the very start of the Six-Day War, we would not be here talking to you; there would be no Israel.

"Yes, we know all that; therefore we are not so mad as to suggest simply turning all those bases back to an enemy that vows to drive us into the sea and destroy us. We do not consider that an idle boast. If the Arabs had won, we would have been drowned in our own blood, not just the sea. Israel is perhaps the only country in the world that cannot afford to lose a war. Others can lose and emerge stronger than ever —Germany, Japan—but that would not be our fate."

This pessimistic and very hardheaded estimate, almost identical with the arguments of the most right-wing advocates of a tough line, came from a very left-wing graduate student in political science, Elie Schurr, age twenty-six. The fundamental facts and arguments are well known and there is widespread agreement, from right to left, on the dangers of concessions for peace.

Where the left-wing minority opposition diverges from right and center is the issue of the long-run danger of a permanent status quo, in which potential frontiers become real frontiers, in which the state of a nation-in-arms becomes a way of life, in which military imperatives replace civilian imperatives, with a consequent disappearance of the original Israeli objective of a humanitarian society, devolving into just another state, with the threat of war forever a current calculation.

The opposition sees this as so great a danger that it feels some risks must be taken now to avoid the nightmare vision of its analysis becoming a new Israeli reality in place of the old dream. To avoid this, they offer a number of alternatives:

Agree to return the occupied territories—always excepting Jerusalem—on certain conditions: strictly contracted and patrolled demilitarization of the Golan, the Gaza Strip, Sharm-el-Sheikh, the Sinai, the West Bank. Israeli patrols and Israeli fortresses to be prominent in the security-control forces and areas.

The creation of a Palestinian state on the West Bank, demilitarized, with close economic and communication bonds with Israel.

Trade and communication accords for transit across Arab and Israel territories, the Suez Canal, and the Red Sea.

A treaty with the United States guaranteeing Israel's security, endorsing these agreements, and participating in their supervision.

Objections can be made, are constantly made, to each and all of these suggestions, as to many other proposals the opposition puts forward. The clear majority of the citizens, including a clear majority of "the children of reality," the new generation of Israel—born citizens—support the government even when grumbling about it.*

* For national opinion poll results on peace negotiations and the territories, see Appendix: Continuing Survey, A1–A10, pp. 234–237.

The views cited above are small minority views. But they are being voiced by more citizens every month and, small as they may be, are too significant now merely to be brushed aside. Sooner or later, and likely sooner, they will force the government to debate its policies and articulate them more clearly—which is a proper role for an opposition, particularly the very loyal opposition of Israel.

The most vehement critics of the government in Israel are not alienated from society or from the state. There is no valid analogy between Israeli youth and the youth movements in other countries. The long-range objective is the creation of a better society, but the overriding concern, unlike that of young Americans or young Frenchmen, is survival. More than that, young Israelis love their country, are proud of it, conceitedly, arrogantly, unashamedly.

American observers of this Israeli scene cannot but feel a terrible sense of loss as they compare Israeli youth with their own. Americans once shared a dream, once believed in their country as the essence of the human state, the hope, the magnet of the world. Our youth, critical of their elders, as each succeeding generation is, was not alienated from society, not even in the worst days of the Depression, that traumatic period of modern history in which today's rulers of American society were young men and women.

Young Americans had few doubts about the justice of their cause in World War II, and we landed on foreign coasts as an army of liberation, not an army of conquest, not as the neo-imperialist vanguard of an anti-communist "crusade," self-righteous defenders of the one true system.

It is true that the majority of young Americans, those who work, study, and do not demonstrate, still have faith in America and do not hate it. That truth does not diminish the terrible loss of the large minority, including some of our best-educated, best-motivated young citizens.

Israel has not paid the high price that America has, despite three wars and long military service. There are two main reasons for the loyalty of Israeli youth.

The state does not ask them to fight for conquest or for a power position in the world or for highly theoretical, largely rhetorical policies. Israel calls upon young Israelis to fight for their homes, their families, their own survival. There is no stronger motivation for national service.

The second reason can be found in the system of military training and service, one of the most democratic, morale-building, and character-building military systems to be found anywhere in the world.

\* \* \*

Our car bucked and bounced over a rocky road, curving up the heights outside Jerusalem, in the stone-strewn hills that are one of the oldest battlegrounds in history, in the lands west of the Jordan River. We were going to an army base in the "administered territories," the Arab-populated lands known as the West Bank.

As we twisted around a cliff, we came upon a sentry post blocking the road, behind it the watchtower of the camp. Our papers were cleared quickly, without formality, and we were moved through with a nod and a wave. An army officer was in the car with us, but neither he nor the sentries bothered to salute. When I asked him why, he was genuinely surprised: "He knows me, I know him; we're not on parade."

We turned in to the main street of the camp, a very wide paved road, naked, glaring in the brutal African sun, un-trimmed with flowers, surrounded by scrub hills.

On the right was the headquarters building, three-story, white stucco, the flag of Israel flying from a mast above the double-doored entrance. On the left a parade ground and drill field, with a platoon of men, surprisingly clothed in wool despite the ninety-degree heat, moving through close-order drill.

From far off, beyond the field, through a purplish heat haze in the hills, came the sound of firing. "Rifle and machine-gun practice," said the officer. "That's the firing range out there."

The camp looked like every field camp I have known as a soldier and war correspondent. It surprised me, for I had heard so much about how different the Israeli Army was that I had come to expect even physical differences. It was not very different, there in the hill country, from my own basic-training camp of many years ago in Fort Dix, New Jersey, except for the absence of Jersey's green trees.

I thought back to those first days at Dix, in what seemed another life, another world, not mine. I smiled—now I can smile—at the memory of the very first line-up of recruits and the tough, professional sergeant who barked out: "All college graduates one pace forward!"

Not having been warned about the maneuver, I stepped forward proudly, assuming I'd be appointed an N.C.O. on the spot. About a dozen bright-faced youngsters stepped forward with me, and we nodded knowingly to each other.

"Now, all those with advanced degrees, another pace forward!"

A half-dozen of the "élite" smartly advanced.

"Okay, you big brains," the sergeant snarled, "advanced degrees to shit-house detail. Get your mops, move your asses, on the double, on the double."

He scowled at the remaining, shaken "élite." "College grads to kitchen police; let's see if you know how to peel potatoes."

"The rest of you guys, ten minutes' break, then line up for drill. Maybe we can make soldiers out of you."

The Israeli lieutenant, our escort officer, howled until he cried with laughter as I told him the story of my introduction to the army.

"Is that really the way it is?" he asked.

"Well, no, not now, I guess. But that's the way it was back in the early forties, when America was thrust into war unprepared and with not much military sophistication. I'm sure it's not that way now."

"Can't be," said the Israeli. "You can't build a good army by breaking the spirit of its men. Just the opposite. The best soldier is the best-motivated soldier, who knows what he is doing and why and is respected by his officers, who themselves must win his respect. This is our principle. We really have no choice, you know. Our population is very small; every man must count to his fullest capacity . . . and beyond, if need be."

We had made our way, by then, to the bureau of the duty officer, a company commander, a captain. He asked for his name to be withheld. "I do not think it wise for field commanders to be closely identified. Call me Yussef; that is close enough."

Yussef is a tall, very thin, but sinewy man, with muscles like coiled springs under a very dark skin. If I did not know that he was an Israeli, I would have taken him for a Bedouin or an Indian. He is, in fact, a Yemenite by birth, but his parents came to Israel when he was two years old.

Yussef is now twenty-seven, married, has a daughter. His family lives two hours away and he goes home to see them three times a week. Army men get frequent passes to go home and can get across the country easily, for distances are not great in Israel.

Israel is a very small country, in size and population roughly the equivalent of the state of Kentucky (which it resembles in no other way). Some 3,000,000 people live in and occupy a territory of some 34,000 square miles of area, most of them in urban centers, with good communications. From Jerusalem on the eastern frontier, to Tel Aviv, the big city of the west, on the Mediterranean, is about a ninety-minute drive across the width of the nation (which gives some idea of its security and defense problems).

Half of the total population lives in the two cities of Jerusalem and Tel Aviv. And if one takes those who live in the four biggest cities, of a hundred thousand population and over, then 85 out of 100 Israelis live in big cities, making Israel, once the land of the pioneer, the most urban society in the world.

It is also one of the most mobile societies in the world. Practically everyone, like Captain Yussef, is going home, hitchhiking across the country, or in his own car. The hours before the Friday Sabbath, on the much-traveled Jerusalem-Tel Aviv highway—one of the most dangerous zones in the world (not because of enemies, but because of the wild Israeli drivers)—are particularly crowded and hazardous.

Soldiers—with their ubiquitous Uzi submachine guns, or rifles, knapsack on back—line the roads thumbing commandingly for lifts. They get frequent Sabbath or weekend passes to visit their families, but must keep their guns with them at all times and be tuned in by transistor radio to newscasts in case of an emergency.

Captain Yussef told us: "It is very good for a soldier to feel close to his family and to be able to visit them. Then he knows what he is defending. And his family knows that he is well and strong and getting stronger in the army. It ties civilians to the army and the army to the civilians. In fact, as everyone will tell you, we are one, the army and the people; there is no separation."

Captain Yussef is one of the many Yemenite Jews who have found a place for themselves in Israel, both in and out of the army. In general, Jews from Yemen find their place swiftly in Israel.

Yussef was educated in a religious seminary, training to be a religious teacher. When drafted, he continued his studies in the army and then applied for officer-training school. He is now committed to military service, as a professional officer, through 1974, in order to take advantage of the army's generous educational and housing allowances. He expects to leave the army at the end of his current term, but is not sure he will go back to the teaching of religion.

"I have learned a lot in the army. I have some new ideas. I'm thinking about it."

*     *     *

Zvika Vikinisky, age nineteen, whose parents came from Argentina, is also thinking about his future, not sure whether he wants to go back to his kibbutz after his army service ends.

"I come from the kibbutz of B'nai Dior, near Netanya. It's a wonderful place. I have been happy there and they helped me a lot. The kibbutz gave me a loan, without interest, of two hundred and fifty pounds a month [about sixty dollars] to help me with my expenses as a student at the Technion, in Haifa. The government has given me scholarships, and now the army will help me continue.

"But if I'm going to be an engineer I may need a bigger scope for my work than my kibbutz can offer. I don't know yet. My parents will leave it up to me.

"My father had ten years of education; my mother is a high school graduate. They want me to go on to higher degrees.

"They didn't suffer in Argentina. They came to Israel so they could live as Jews in a Jewish land. That's Zionism.

"Zionism should be distinguished from religious Judaism. Zionism is political and social. Of course, the basic drive is freedom for Jews. But then it is up to Jews to interpret Judaism for themselves. In this sense, I am a Zionist.

"We should keep the gates of Israel open for all Jews, encourage and aid immigration, but, of course, with a deliberate pace. We could be overwhelmed by waves of immigration. Russian Jews we must take care of, at whatever cost, for that is an emergency. But Jews from other lands can be scheduled with the problems in mind of new jobs, homes, and so on. I think government policy on this is right.

"I know some of us sabras complain, particularly the Oriental Jews, that everything is given to the *olim,* the new immigrants, while they are the forgotten men, born here, so nothing is done for them. There is some truth to this. But we cannot turn Jews away.

"The acculturation process for Jews from so many different lands is difficult, of course, but after all we are all Jews; that is a powerful linking force. And the army is an excellent melting pot, an acculturation crucible for all Israelis.

"I have no opinion on the war in Vietnam. That's your problem. My problem is to keep Israel free. On this, I think your American policy has been most helpful. We'd like more help—sure, who wouldn't? But you have been very good and we are grateful.

"What I want is a normal life, to work as an engineer, to be married at twenty-five, and to have at least three children. That's all. But it's a lot."

*   *   *

Private Moty Fogel, like Zvika, is a student at Technion, nineteen years old, born in Israel of immigrant parents. His parents came as refugees from Poland after World War II. His father was a merchant, not highly educated.

Moty was born in Tel Aviv, the family's third son. His eldest brother is an army career officer; the middle brother is a student at Tel Aviv University. Moty was in his first year at Technion when the army call came. He will keep up his studies in the army, go back to Technion to take his degree as an electrical engineer. Then he wants to get married when he is twenty-three.

"It's good to get married young, have children—I'd like three—and grow up with your children."

Co-author Lucy Szekely asked what qualities he sought in a wife.

"Well, she should be younger than I—a few years. A good girl and not stupid."

Lucy raised an eyebrow, smiled, and asked, "Not stupid? Do you consider women stupid?"

"No, I wouldn't say that," Moty protested. "What I mean is she doesn't have to be very intelligent."

Moty paused, realizing he was getting into trouble.

"I mean, it's all right if she's intelligent. That would be nice. But that's not so important. I mean, a good girl, a good wife, who wants kids and will be a good mother."

Like most young men, particularly those planning to get married, Moty was concerned about housing shortages. But he thought the government was doing just about as well as could be expected given the demands of the defense forces and the needs of the new immigrants.

When we asked him about new luxury housing and the profits of speculators, he seemed unaware of any such scandal and inclined to doubt our information.

"The newspapers make a scandal of everything. They talk more about housing than they should." Sensing our surprise, he added, with a sly smile, "Of course, I believe in freedom of the press. They should not be prohibited from writing what they think."

Moty told us that his maternal grandfather was a rabbi and that his parents were religious but that he is not, nor are his brothers.

"We obey the kosher laws, but that's more from tradition, convenience, and respect for our parents than from religious convictions. I believe that religion stands in the way of modern progress."

Moty said, "It's all right with me if kosher laws are maintained by state laws. I know a lot of people do not believe in the dietary laws, but why offend our rabbis and those who do believe? You can get enough to eat kosher. We eat kosher and very well in the army."

Moty did not think this was a contradiction of his statement that religion stands in the way of modern progress.

"No, where it stands in the way, it must be stopped. Modern progress is more important. But I can be the world's best engineer and still eat kosher."

Moty also thought that divorce should not be allowed. But he conceded that this was a highly conservative stand and very controversial.

"It ought to be debated and change come about slowly. That is the best way. Slowly. By consent of the majority."

As he and the other soldiers spoke, it was difficult for us to remember that they were nineteen and twenty years old. They sounded twice their age.

When asked what territories, which he was defending, might be given up for real peace, Moty thought a moment and then answered: "Real peace? Those are words. I would be willing to give up everything we won in 1967." He hastily added, "Except Jerusalem, of course.

"But that's all theory right now. Today a return of territories would simply lead to a renewal of war. These territories are and have been springboards for invasion against us. Many of us have died because of attacks launched from this West Bank, from the Golan Heights, the Gaza Strip, from Sinai. We soldiers who hold these lands now know what we are holding and why. By and large, we support our government's policy.

"We hear a lot of talk about the Palestinian question. Should there be a Palestinian state? Well, that's their problem, not ours. Are the Arabs really one nation, as they claim? No, they are more different from each other than the surface similarities among them. Did we stop them from making a Palestinian state? We made our state in 1948. Why didn't they make theirs?"

To find out how these opinions compared with the national average, we consulted the national Continuing Survey on two questions:

CONTINUING SURVEY:

QUESTION A1—In your opinion, are the Arab countries presently disposed to speak about a *real peace* with Israel?

|  | Youth | Adults |
|---|---|---|
|  | % | % |
| Absolutely | 1 | 2 |
| Perhaps | 16 | 18 |
| No, not yet | 66 | 66 |
| Less now than ever | 17 | 14 |
|  | 100 | 100 |

CONTINUING SURVEY:

QUESTION A6—Concerning the territories occupied by Israel since the Six-Day War, which, in your opinion, is the greatest concession to be made to reach a peace agreement with the Arab countries?

|  | Youth | Adults |
|---|---|---|
|  | % | % |
| Give up all the territories | 1 | 1 |
| Give up almost all the territories | 6 | 2 |
| Give up part of the territories | 25 | 28 |
| Give up a small part of the territories | 39 | 40 |
| Don't give up anything at all | 29 | 29 |
|  | 100 | 100 |

Once again, as we found in nearly every survey on almost every major issue, there is an astonishing symmetry of views between young and old. This does not mean, as our own interviews in depth and at length showed, that there is not a generation gap. There are real differences in culture, ideology, and life style between the children of reality, and the fathers of the dream. But on the major political issues of the day these differences are not operative. Israel's government is one of the most solid in the world when it comes to democratic support for its major policies.

Dr. Elie Kenan, sociologist of Hebrew University and senior staff member of the Institute, warns, however, not to give absolute weight to the Survey findings.

"Polls constitute a photograph of the opinions of the ensemble of the population, with the opinions of different respondents all having equal weight. In this way, polls differ from the realities of public and political life where the opinions of certain groups, often minority groups (intellectuals, extremists, activists, and so on), resound more strongly. Thus the statistical opinions of youth, as expressed in the studies, correspond to the ensemble of youth in the population and not necessarily to certain minorities who express themselves more frequently and forcefully. The 'silent majority' gets equal time in polls."

Abraham Lincoln once polled his Cabinet on a project he proposed and the entire Cabinet voted no. Lincoln looked around the table and said "I vote aye." He paused and added, "The 'ayes' have it."

In this sense, it is unlikely to matter what the polls show about peace negotiations with the Arabs or about what territories Israel will annex or return and under what conditions. Golda Meir, as a strong-willed and popularly supported Prime Minister, holds a powerful "aye" vote for any solution that she favors.

The Prime Minister made her views forcefully clear in an interview published in the paper *Ma'ariv* on September 9, 1972. Although her statement was published after the massacre of the Jewish Olympic team, it had been recorded by the paper before that, and received even more popular acclaim because of the anti-Palestinian rage unleashed by the odious murders.

"We won't go back to the old borders of 1967, with just small changes," said the Prime Minister. "There must be big changes. The Arabs must know that peace will be achieved when they are ready to give up territory."

Mrs. Meir disposed bluntly of the objection that there are 600,000 Arabs on the West Bank, whose numbers would change the nature of the Jewish state if they were absorbed into it.

She told *Ma'ariv:* "Israel wants only a minimum of Arab population in the Jordanian territory it wishes to keep." Her use of the phrase "Jordanian territory" indicated that she is still adamantly opposed to the notion of creating a Palestinian state. She prefers to deal with King Hussein, the Arab leader most favorable to peace with Israel and most hostile to the Palestinians who seek to overthrow his rule.

At the same time that the *Ma'ariv* interview appeared, another paper, *Yediot Aharanot,* printed an interview in Amman by an unidentified adviser to King Hussein, who quoted the monarch as saying that he "not only wants peace with Israel, but is, in fact, very interested in it."

Hussein was quoted as saying that Israel is now a permanent, indigenous force in the Middle East.

"In 1948, we were dealing with Jewish émigrés from Europe. Now more than fifty percent of Israelis were born in Israel. Where are they to go? Whether the Arabs like it or not, now they must make peace with Israel."

# VIII

## Of Men and Arms

*So were all those that were numbered of the children of Israel, by the house of their fathers, from twenty years old and upward, all that were able to go forth to war in Israel. . . .*

—NUMBERS 1:45.

I N modern history, Jews are more likely to figure as scholars, scientists, musicians, financiers, or merchants than as
warriors. One has to go back to the Bible to read about the
martial skills and valor of the Hebrew peoples. Yet, even in
modern history, a Jew played an important role in military
affairs, as the innovator of the system of the citizen-soldier
rather than the professional mercenary.

It was Lazare Carnot, a deputy of the French Revolution, who first advanced and put into practice the notion of
"a nation-in-arms." Every citizen physically fit to bear arms
was declared to be at the service of the state—a truly revolutionary concept. Ever since the eighteenth century, Carnot's
concept has been adopted universally, although not necessarily democratically.

It is, perhaps fittingly, in a Jewish state that this theory of
a nation-in-arms has reached its highest aims and known its
finest hour. Jews are not a martial people and have not had
a military tradition since ancient times. This is true in Israel
today, which demands more personal service to the military
and spends more per capita of its income on defense than
any other country in the world. The miracle of Israel is that
it has achieved so extraordinary a degree of militarization
without having become militaristic. The army is at the service
of the state, under very tight civilian control, with a political
role much smaller than its swollen ranks and budgets would
give it in other nations.

A few basic figures reveal the incredible size and weight
of defense budgets. One can imagine easily their impact on
every citizen of Israel when one knows how onerous the
military burden is in the United States, the richest country in
the world, with a per-capita military expenditure far less than
that of the Israelis. (Defense expenditures amount to 31%

of Israel's gross national product, compared with less than 10% in the U.S.A.)

Israel's total defense expenses increased, from 1971 to 1972 (a year of "peace"), by 18%, to a total of $2,000,000,-000. Since the population is only some 3,000,000 people, this means that every single citizen of Israel spent, statistically, $666.66 for national defense. In America, with a much higher per-capita income, the defense burden is less than $400 per citizen.

National defense has become costlier than war itself. In the years since the Six-Day War, actual defense costs have multiplied five times, particularly because of the extremely high costs of American planes and modern sophisticated weapons.

Defense costs, plus debt service, consume more than Israel's total tax revenue. No other country in the world bears such a burden or anything even close to it. Defense budgets alone consume 80% of tax revenues, 32% of imports, and 25% of Israel's manpower. As a result, Israel's foreign-currency debt, a very heavy mortgage on the young generation's future, has already passed a total of $3,500,000,000, making it a debt of more than $1,000 per citizen, the highest, by far, in the world (seven times higher than the next country on the debt list).

"It's an awful waste of time, the worst thing a man can do. Yes, the army is an evil—a necessary evil, but an evil. It is antihuman. It is chauvinist, divides people and nations. If only one day the peoples of the world could find the way to live without arming to the teeth, and breaking their backs with the burden of arms."

The man who spoke these words is a high-ranking general, Shlomo Lahat, then Chief of Army Manpower. General Lahat—"Tcheetch"—a short, stocky, heavy-shouldered man, almost as broad as he is high, put two big fists on his desk and said, "I am a soldier by profession but not a professional soldier. I am really a civilian, a farmer who had to leave the land to take up arms because I had to, not because I wanted to.

"I do not see life through the periscope of a tank. I see death through the periscope of a tank. But my tanks had to sweep through the Sinai to keep death from the gates of Israel. This is true of almost all our officers and soldiers. Every man up to fifty-five must do his three years' service on active duty and at least forty days a year in reserve training. That's why we say, 'An Israeli soldier is a citizen with forty days' duty a year.' Or a citizen is a soldier with eleven months' annual leave from the army. We are, truly, a nation-at-arms."

Tcheetch paused, ran his hands across his stubble of blond-gray hair, and frowned.

"It would be easy, you know, to become a militaristic state in these conditions. Except that we are not militarists. Our parents did not come to Palestine to found a military state, nor were we raised with militaristic ideas. We were raised in the mythology of the nobility of closeness to the soil, of the socialist ideology and the desperate need of Jews for a homeland.

"We began with self-defense brigades linking farms and settlements. Out of this grew a revolutionary force, then the official armed forces. We were not inducted into an army, taught military tactics and theory, indoctrinated with military traditions, as in other countries. We had to learn our own tactics, suitable for our own land and the nature of the threat to our homes. We had no West Point, no military institutes. Some of our forefathers served in the Turkish Army; our fathers served in the British Army. But most of all we had to create the Israeli Army by ourselves. Like your American Minutemen, your farmers at Lexington.

"Our tradition, our temperament, right through the entire corps is civilian. That is why, despite the weight of the military, our army is the democratic servant of the state, its men citizens in uniform. Not professionals." He grinned, lifted his head proudly, and added, "Not that we're a bunch of amateurs. We have one hell of an army."

A soldier came in with documents for the General, a very attractive, black-haired young woman in her twenties. As she walked out of the office, General Lahat commented, "We don't believe in immobilizing men with office work. The girls are better at it anyway. But we don't use women just for office work. And even the women office workers are trained in fundamental skills. Our girls can use guns, too.

"We have found that women have a special aptitude for psychiatric work, particularly applied techniques of psychiatric training and job interviewing. We test everyone who enters the army, in a series of examinations and interviews for a full month, before basic training begins. In that month, we try to find out just where a man is best suited. For example, if we find someone with a passion for neatness and orderliness, we assign him to a tank, where maximum efficient use of small space is required.

"In this first month, we sort out the girls with the highest I.Q.s and quiet personalities. They are put into a special three-month training course by our professional psychiatrists to prepare them for psychiatric testing and interviewing of recruits. They serve for twenty months, and some of them are then promoted to assistant psychiatrists, with higher rank and pay, and serve an additional six months as volunteers beyond the draft term itself.

"The law permits us to draft women for twenty-four months' service but we believe that twenty months is optimum. If they do not want to serve at all and object to being drafted, we don't take them. We do get objections, particularly from religious families. As for the men, in all of last year we only had twelve conscientious objectors.

"We have a bigger problem with youngsters who are not physically fit but who want to serve. Our policy is to take them if they are mentally healthy and if they can walk and take care of themselves. There are lots of duties that can be performed by the physically handicapped, useful to us and, above all, vital to the individual's self-respect and confidence.

"Survival is our prime objective but the individual is our prime concern. To serve in the Israeli Army is not just a service, a duty; it is a culture. As a general in charge of manpower, it is not my assignment to provide human parts to a military machine, but to train a citizen to defend his home and make him a more useful, better-educated citizen in his civilian life. Then not only will Israel be well defended but our society will be stronger and healthier. That's the philosophy of the Israeli Army.

"Military observers come from around the world. They want to find the 'secret' of our success. There is no secret. It's all out in the open. We have the best-trained, best-motivated armed force, with the highest morale of any in the world." General Lahat laughed and added, "And we're modest, too."

His orderly came in with a tray of tea and cookies. He looked down at his waistline—still trim—and pushed the cookies toward me. I looked down at mine—not trim enough —and pushed them back to him. He broke one in half, offered it to me, and we both gobbled our halves down.

"Discipline can be imposed but fighting spirit must be generated. It is highest when motivated by a love for freedom. But freedom is a feeling. You can't dictate how a man should feel. That is why there is free discussion all through our training. We are very responsive to complaints and to suggestions. Some of the best ideas we have came from the ranks and sometimes from raw recruits.

"Our greatest success, our pride and joy, is also in some respects one of our headaches—a good headache, mind you. It is the prestige of the élite corps: pilots, paratroopers, submariners, and frogmen. That's what every Israeli boy wants to be. These are volunteer units and the lists are subscribed ten times over. It's tough to weed them out, for we have many excellent candidates and sometimes it is heartbreaking to see a boy who put everything into it get turned down. And we have to guard against the very idea of élite units. Every soldier is equally valuable to his country. A pilot is not a better man than a foot soldier. Sure, it's more glamorous to be a paratrooper than a slogger, but glamour is a dangerous drug. We do not want and will not have swashbucklers in the democratic army of Israel."

The General called in his orderly, then said, "Look at his uniform, feel the cloth. Now look at mine. Same cloth, same cut, for the private and the general. Only our insignia are different—and see how small they are. We do not tell our soldiers to respect the uniform, not the man. In our army, every man, of any rank, wins or loses respect by his own ability, not his tailor's."

Tcheetch got up, suggested that our wives check out a dinner appointment—"There's a fantastic French-Tunisian restaurant in town. Jewish, but not kosher"—and added, in farewell, "Soon I'll be leaving the army and looking for a job —going back to civilian life at last. That's another democratic safeguard against a military establishment. Almost all top officers—the very highest—leave service at age fifty, or younger. We are a young nation; we want a young army, and no dug-in vested interests."

General Lahat kept talking as he escorted me out of his office and to my car. I felt that it was not so much to convince me but rather an outflow of ideas from his own passion for his subject.

"One of the reasons for our high budgets is that we are not rich enough to buy cheap. We can't order in quantity at lowest prices. We need quality, whether it is material or men.

"The thing to remember is that there is a broad national consensus in Israel, and out of it comes the general acceptance of the burden and the readiness to fight if fight we must. Our slogan, of the entire nation, is *'Ain Brera'*—'We Have No Choice!' We must fight for our homes, freedoms, and lives. No more exiles, no more ghettos, no more concentration camps, no more ovens!

"But we know that if we have to fight again, the main burden will fall upon our youth. Therefore we must conduct ourselves in such a manner that youth knows that it will not be called to arms because of some elder's pride, or stubbornness.

"If youth wants us to give up territories and we find that it can be done without grave peril, but with risks, then we will have to take risks, for the morale of our youth and our responsibility toward the men we must call to battle is paramount."

\*     \*     \*

Brigadier General Izthak Arad, head of the army's Department of Education, agreed largely with what Tcheetch had said, but added, "The army doesn't deserve all the credit for the high morale of the troops. It arises out of the family and cultural background in which our young generation has been raised.

"Recruits come to us with the advance knowledge that their service is not only a national duty but a personal imperative. We do not have to indoctrinate them to danger. They have known nothing but danger from the day the state was declared, from the day they were born.

"Many parents will tell you, as will many young people— I'm sure you hear it over and over again—that the holocaust is ancient history or that Hitler is a figure almost as meaningless now as Torquemada. Don't you believe it. It is fashionable to say things like this. Youth looks ahead, not backwards. They're concerned about how to make peace with Sadat, not Hitler, so they pretend to be unimpressed with the past. But they know, they know, because their parents talk about it, because relatives died in concentration camps, and others who survived still bear the physical and psychological scars and live among us.

"The holocaust, Hitler—they are living, not dead memories, and deep down our youth knows it would be spared no quarter, no humiliation, no torture, not life itself were Israel not strong enough, ready enough to defend its gates. This is not in the foreground of many young people but it is very much high in the background. And that is what the army builds on in its education and morale programs."

General Arad is a war-toughened veteran of the Red Army of Russia. Born and raised in Lithuania, he fought with the Soviets against Hitler's invading armies. Then, in 1945, at the end of the war, he emigrated to Israel to fight for his own state, his own people, "and for myself; that is very important, to fight for oneself, too.

"I didn't come to Israel because a law ordered me to. I didn't join the army and fight for our independence because there was a law. And our youth does not enter our army because of a universal military service law. We train, we fight because we have to and because we believe in our cause. This gives each man the strength of ten who fight for other, lesser reasons.

"Our youth is different from its parents in that it is not doctrinaire, not theoretical, not dogmatic. I'm in very close touch with the troops and I know that they believe mainly what they can see, touch, and feel. They know that their officers want peace as much as they do. They know we do not consider ourselves saints and the Arabs devils. That's not a Jewish concept.

"We recognize Arab rights and Arab motivations. We seek coexistence. The other side has said no to every reasonable proposal made and our men know this. But we are patient. More proposals will be made and one day there will be peace. Meantime, we're all right, heavy though the burden may be.

"We see ourselves, beyond Israel, as the true center of Jewish existence in the world, as the sole guarantor of Jewish existence in the long run, so we are fighting for something not only essential to ourselves but greater than ourselves, and we often talk of this in troop educational programs.

"Before the Second World War, the vital area of Jewish existence for centuries was in Europe, but today there are three new centers in the world: Israel, the reservoir; America and Russia, the feed-streams.

"In America there appears to be an increasing curve of assimilation as the generations evolve. Jewish youth, over all, has been losing its sense of identity with Jewish 'nationality.' Sure there are many dedicated young Jews—thank God—in America, but we would be criminally blind not to recognize an over-all erosion, and a sharp increase in mixed marriages. Why, I am told that among Jewish college graduates mixed marriages amount to almost forty percent. And each mixed marriage sees a weakening of Jewish identity.

"Assimilation is a powerful force in American society. In the long run, the American Jewish community may grow smaller, less dedicated to Israel, although today it is one of the pillars of world Jewry and of our strength. But we must plan ahead and ask ourselves will it always be?

"As for Russia, the three million Jews in the Soviet Union are fighting a desperate struggle for Jewish existence. Jews are repressed, suppressed, persecuted in the Soviet Union. American assimilation proceeds democratically, with subtle societal and cultural pressures. There is nothing subtle about Soviet assimilation. It is brutal, deliberate, unrelenting.

"This leaves Israel the lodestar of the Jewish universe, the true center of Judaism. Perhaps I would not resent this isolation if the whole world was destroying all religions and all cultural differences to create a new brotherhood of man. But that is not what is happening. And I do not want to see Jewishness alone wiped out in the world.

"I don't want to be in the generation responsible for the end of Jewish history. Our young men and our young women feel the same as I do. Whatever generational differences there may be—and there always are some—this is not one of them. All generations in Israel are aware they are fighting for the continued existence of their faith, their ethics, their culture.

"When we fight, we know exactly what we are fighting for and have no doubts about the justice of our cause. In this, our youth is different from Russian boys sent to Prague or Americans to South Vietnam. That difference is enormous. It shows up in every aspect of our training program."

Once again, an orderly came in with a tray of tea and cookies. I have been a war correspondent in most parts of the world, but never have I seen so many cookies served as in the Israeli Army. American generals serve coffee from the minute one sits down, and if all goes well, there is the hope of a bottle of bourbon and branch water near or at the end. (The coffee is always too hot and too weak, the bourbon and water too strong and too cold). But in Israel it's always cookies. (I wonder if their mothers make them?)

General Arad paid no attention to the tea or the cookies. He was intent on explaining the education of Israel's youth in the army.

"The main condition of life is struggle, constant struggle, in peace or in war. So we help prepare our youth for the struggle of life by giving them a thorough, tough, demanding, and challenging training. But we do not, as some armies do, try to break them down, to crush the individual spirit, in order, so the theory goes, to make them parts of a machine, to make them react instantly to commands, to turn a civilian into a soldier. We do not believe in this theory of orders, formal discipline, automatic reactions.

"Humans are not machines and do not function well automatically, nor can they reintegrate usefully into civilian life if so trained. We think too much formal discipline is bad.

We put a high value on good human communications between officers and men. Above all, we think men function better if they understand not only the mechanics of tactics and strategy but the reasons underlying it. Our men must be knowledgeable and motivated—not commanded, not robots. An officer must not only tell a soldier what to do and how to do it but, more importantly, why it has to be done.

"We live together, train together, wear exactly the same uniforms, and eat exactly the same food. And we have open forum discussions in which everything and anything is up for criticism, challenge, and comment. Listen, it's no Utopia. We have our problems. But, as I told you, life is a problem and our armed forces take their place in the scheme of life and not as a thing apart.

"The second important factor in our training is the principle of personal example. Our slogan is not 'Go forward' but 'Follow me.' The officer is at the head of his troops at all times, and must be able and ready to do everything better than his men. Our commanders are always 'up front.' As a matter of fact, so is the whole country. We have no rear areas in war in Israel.

"In the Six-Day War, of eight hundred men killed two hundred were officers. I led my own battalion through a minefield, not only to set an example but for my own conscience. I could not order men to risk their lives unless I first risked mine.

"I am not a hero and mine is not a unique case. That's what our officers are like. Not all of them, of course. Men are men and some fail. But when they fail we have others to take their place quickly. Promotion is not by seniority but by ability and performance. There aren't enough of us to afford to carry failures.

"The third and most important part of the army program of training for life is our educational program, unique in the world.

"We believe that every young man and woman should complete with passing standards a minimum of a primary education: eight years of studies. Some of those who enter the army have not completed such a course. They come from new immigrants, who have great trouble with Hebrew, or that percentage of our own young sabras who are backward, either because of not very high intelligence or poor home conditions, particularly those who come from the slums and those who have been smoking pot and dropping out. Yes, yes, we have that problem. I told you we're not Utopia.

"Now, what do we do? First, we have instituted a unique pretesting and training program even before they get into the army. Last year we began preinduction courses of six weeks in Hebrew. Then, in the army, we continue the Hebrew lessons during active service. It is vital for society that all citizens attain high literacy in the national language. After three years in the army, every soldier can read and write with fluency. No one will leave the army without a high standard of Hebrew and a basic primary education.

"In the last three months of service, we send those who are still not up to standard to take the intensive course at the David Marcus School, where study conditions are excellent—no slums, no pot, no bitterness, no distractions.

"There is a powerful motivation to succeed, for all these boys want to go at least to vocational schools, to get married, to earn a living. And they can't count on it without earning their certificates and passing national standard exams. Boys with real drive and ability, who came to us underprivileged and backward, make real progress. Ninety-five percent of the men earn their primary education certificates. How's that for a record?

"Some go beyond this and win their certificates of ten years' study. They get special intensive courses at the Marcus School, where we have found that in four months of intensive study a man can make up as much as two years of normal schooling in civilian life. One reason, of course, is the good condition in which they live in the army compared with the problems of family life. Another reason is that they are older in the army, are maturing, are becoming men, not kids, and can study at a faster, more successful pace.

"Why, right now in Tel Aviv, we have two hundred soldiers going to evening high schools, preparing their government exams for secondary school diplomas. Of course, soldiers in combat units can't do this, but they can, and do, sign up for correspondence courses, and we hold educational sessions in active units everywhere. Thousands of soldiers did their homework in the trenches even during the heavy shelling in the period of the War of Attrition before the cease-fire.

"So three years of army service is not a waste of time in Israel. We do not drain society or alienate our youth. We feed society and motivate our youth.

"No one enters our army as an officer. Everyone comes in as a private, then advances to noncommissioned-officer school and officer-training school, up the ranks by ability and performance—no privileged classes. As their individual characteristics manifest themselves, they are sorted out into general units or specialist units: signal corps, intelligence, and so on. We keep them intellectually challenged and we keep them busy—not peeling potatoes or picking up butts, not that kind of army game. We can't waste men.

"We can't waste women, either. The only differences between our treatment of men and women is that we avoid using women for combat duties and we don't take low-standard women into service. If they have a low I.Q. or have been backward in their studies, we do not want them. We don't have enough teachers to give intensive education to all men and all women, so we just don't take women if they're a problem.

"Discrimination? Well, in theory I suppose so. But we

don't have time or means for such theories. We don't want women with problems and we don't want hardened criminals.

"A couple of years ago, we experimented with a rehabilitation program for boys who had criminal records. Too many of them committed crimes in the army, from petty thievery to crimes of violence. Let the police and social workers take care of them, not the army. We've got enough to do for those who deserve it and can make it.

"We really have the most extensive as well as intensive program ever attempted, not only for the backward and underprivileged but the bright ones, too. We don't forget a man because he is up to standard; we help him increase up to his full ability. Why, every year hundreds of regular officers are sent to universities to get their degrees, and we pay everything for them and also give them their full army pay. That's how I went to university, as an officer. I could not have made it without the army.

"Nine out of ten Israelis serve in the army in the most impressionable years of their lives, eighteen to twenty-one. The base is as broad as the population, utterly democratic. The army service is not a necessary, burdensome duty; it is an exciting, maturing experience.

"Mao has explained the success of the Chinese Red Army resulting from the troops 'swimming like fish in the waters of the people.' That's a striking image and a good idea. But I think we can say something simpler, less deliberately political. In Israel, the army is the people and the people are the sovereign power. That is the glory, the strength, the dignity of Israel."

# I X

## Black Panthers
## and White Jews

Have we not all one father? hath not one
God created us? why do we deal treacher-
ously every man against his brother, by pro-
faning the covenant of our fathers?
—MALACHI 2:10.

ALL through history there have been persistent legends about cities of gold. Even in modern times, immigrants to the United States at the turn of this century believed literally that the streets of New York were paved in gold. They found out soon enough that New York's streets were not only not paved in gold, many of them were not paved at all, and it was the immigrant who was expected to take on the job of paving them.

Only one city in the world really looks like a city of gold and that is Jerusalem. When the rising and setting sun lights up the golden-tinted stone of the ancient city, a glittering gold mirage arises from the streets and houses. It is a dazzling sight that people never tire of seeing, particularly those who live in the better residential districts of Jerusalem.

But there are fifty thousand citizens of Jerusalem for whom the golden mirage is not only an illusion of light but a constant bitter reminder of their own plight. They live in the slum district of Musrara, a breeding ground of crime, drugs, violence, and social conflicts—nothing even close to the horrors of Bedford-Stuyvesant, Harlem or the East Bronx, or the giant slums of Newark, Philadelphia, Washington, Detroit, Chicago, and other points around the compass of American urban nightmares. But since prosperity and poverty are weighed by men on relative rather than absolute scales—the American slum dweller seeing great wealth and comfort around him feels more deprived than the Bushman who knows only his own condition—the grievances of the Jerusalem slum dweller are deeply felt no matter how much better off he is than the slum dweller in Casablanca or Bombay or Harlem.

Unfortunately, someone—very likely an American New Left immigrant, with a flair for publicity—had the bright idea of giving the name Black Panthers to a group of rebellious youth in the Musrara slums. Throughout the year 1971, stories about the Black Panthers of Israel mushroomed around the world.

Jews, particularly those most active in support of Israel, were dismayed. Among intellectual left-wing Jews in America—many of them partisans of the Arab cause and angry critics of Israel—voices were raised to denounce the "crimes" of Israeli "capitalism." There is among Jews, as one can find in all peoples who have long suffered persecution, oppression, and humiliation, a strain of self-hatred that can make people vicious enemies of their own kind.

In Israel itself, the reaction was one of shock and shame, followed swiftly by demands that the "Pantherim" be heard and that their grievances be fairly considered and treated. In interview after interview, we heard young men and women, from left to right, say essentially this: "The grievances dramatized by the Black Panthers are real and must be dealt with, even though the Panther leaders and spokesmen are not truly representative of the problem; they misstate it, exaggerate it, and do their own cause harm because they themselves are disreputable petty criminals and dropouts."

The main charge of the Pantherim was that of discrimination, even racial discrimination. Some of their press releases read as though they had been written in America. And, in fact, American sociologists, such as Dr. Naomi Kies of M.I.T., were close friends and advisers of the Panthers.

The basis of the charge? That although they were Jews, entitled to full equality under the law, they were Jews of an underprivileged, even a despised class, Jews born in Africa or Asia, or native-born of Afro-Asian parents. This is the group of Jews known in Hebrew as Sephardim.

In percentage of total population in Israel, the Sephardim are the majority, a narrow majority of just over 50%. But they are clearly a minority group in terms of education, housing, jobs, social status, and political influence. Israel's affairs, from the days of the pioneers through the founding and first quarter-century of the state, have largely been controlled by the Ashkenazim, the "western" Jew, of Russian, European, American origin.

The tourist industry, the farms and plantations that raise citrus crops, the diamond-cutting industry—the top three dollar-earning businesses—are all in the hands of Jews of European origin. Banks, commerce, the schools are all run by Ashkenazic Jews. Some Syrian, Indian, and Iraqi Jews, prosperous or solid middle-class merchants with a long tradition and experience, have become highly successful members of Israeli society, but, by and large, the Sephardim are poor peasants, lower-middle-class shopkeepers, and make up the mass of unskilled workers at the bottom of the social pyramid. As for the government of Israel, it has been from the start virtually the exclusive preserve of Russian and Eastern European Jews, with only token representation of the Sephardic majority.

No one, not even the government spokesmen, denies the dominant and privileged position of the Ashkenazic Jew and no one denies the grievances of the Sephardim. What is denied most vehemently is the charge of deliberate discrimination, particularly the most shocking of all the Panther charges, that of racial discrimination.

"This charge is so absurd it hardly deserves an answer," asserted David Landor, of the Prime Minister's office.

"The so-called Black Panthers are not black in any sense, neither the pigment of their skin nor their political and economic status in Israel. The title is a propaganda stunt—very clever, with shock value—but absolutely wrong if they mean to imply, as the press has picked it up, that they are a special racial group, politically and socially repressed, as in the United States.

"In fact, they are members of the same subgroup of hu-

mans as the Ashkenazic Jews. They can and do intermarry—
I think the latest figures show almost twenty percent of all
marriages are between young men and women from European
and Afro-Asian families.

"There is a current joke in Israel that the Ashkenazic-
Sephardic issue will be solved in bed. In the long run, that
is true, although it is an oversimplification. It will also be
solved in school and in the army, the two great cultural cruci-
bles of our society.

"Our biggest problem after military security—and, in the
long run, our biggest problem of all—is to prevent the development of two Israels: one rich, powerful, of European
culture; the other poor, weak, of Oriental culture. Those who
say it is inevitable are wrong; those who assert it cannot possibly happen are also wrong. It is not inevitable; in some
ways it already exists, but it can, must, and will be corrected
if we frankly recognize the nature of the problem and set
about liquidating it."

Eliezer Shavit is one of the Israeli leaders who have recognized the problem and are doing something about it. He is
an official of the International Education Foundation, an
organization that has raised $35,000,000 since 1965 for an
Israeli "Headstart" program for children from Oriental—
that is, Afro-Asian—families.

I.E.F. has built 80 kindergartens and prekindergarten
schools, for children three to five, providing facilities for some
6,000 children. It has also built 40 secondary schools, while
50 more are now under construction. The state provides free
and compulsory primary education from age five through
nine years. Secondary education is not compulsory and not
free. Organizations like I.E.F. have been created to provide
free preschool nurseries and kindergartens and free or nom-
inal secondary education, including free meals and all-day
care for children of disadvantaged families and crowded
homes.

It is in the crowded homes of the Jews from Oriental cultures that the trouble begins. It is not unusual to find families of eight and ten living in two small rooms. There is no quiet place for the child to study. He is driven to the streets, where gangs form rapidly and drugs are readily available, particularly since "kif" or "hash" has long been common in Arab countries.

More than half of all the children entering elementary school come from families of Afro-Asian culture, but only ten out of a hundred entering high school are Afro-Asian Jews, and in college the percentage drops below five. Inevitably, Jews from European homes get the best jobs and become entrenched leaders of Israeli society and politics. They start with an advantage, for their parents are better educated, can help them with their homework, give them a quiet corner to work in at home. The advantage gets bigger and wider as the children of European parents advance to college and to postgraduate work on higher degrees.

Not only is the level of education higher among Jews of European origin, but the nature of the education they received in their nations of origin before immigration was Western and modern, whereas among Afro-Asian Jews, even those who are well educated, the emphasis was on literature and law, on the ancient Hebrew texts, with little stress on science or mathematics.

Ironically one of the difficulties for the Sephardic Jews arose not out of discrimination against them, as the Panthers charge, but out of a refusal to discriminate against them. Dr. Abraham Minkowich, Professor of Education at the Hebrew University of Jerusalem, told us how David Ben-Gurion laid down the strictest rules for "unitary education" on the founding of the state.

"We are one people," Ben-Gurion said, "free at last, free of all prejudice and discrimination. We must obliterate all differences, with no distinction between secular and socialist schools, and hold down to the tightest minimum differences between state and religious institutions." Ben-Gurion conceded that there must be some autonomy and some differences in curriculum allowed religious seminaries, just as technical and vocational schools required special courses. But a fundamental curriculum must be followed by all schools.

"Ben-Gurion and other leaders," said Professor Minkowich, "assumed that all Jewish boys and girls would be good students." The Professor laughed. "Who ever heard of a backward Jewish student?"

He paused and added, "But we do have many students who need special attention, not necessarily because they are stupid or retarded—although that is a human problem that appears everywhere—but because many youngsters of perfectly good brains and learning ability suffer from bad homes, bad housing, cultural shock, and any number of other impedimenta to normal learning progress. This is a key factor in the problem of children from some Afro-Asian families. And they suffered not from discrimination but from lack of discrimination, because Ben-Gurion wanted to treat them the same as everyone else, not understanding they needed special treatment."

We were seated in the faculty lounge of Hebrew University, in a large hacienda-style ranch room, very much like the lounges in the universities of southern California. The Professor had ordered cold beer, sandwiches, and cigarettes. Practically everyone was smoking. Although it was a brilliantly sunny day, with the translucent light of Jerusalem shining on the golden stones, the faculty lounge was fogged in with blue-gray swirling clouds of smoke.

"At the beginning, back in 1948, we could not see the dimensions this problem would take on. At that time, only a third of the population were sabras. Two-thirds were immigrants, mainly from Eastern Europe and Russia. It seemed natural enough to adopt a curriculum and teaching methods based upon Eastern European and German traditions and doctrines.

"There was strong emphasis on verbal learning, on memory and rote. On what we call 'frontal teaching.' And there were some fringe progressive methods, such as group discussion. Well, with children from literate, educated, articulate families—and this was the case with many of the immigrant Ashkenazim—with a strong socioeconomic background, it all worked very well.

"Then, in the early fifties, came a giant wave of Jewish immigrants from the Arab lands of the Middle East and from the crisis-ridden revolutionary countries of French North Africa, particularly from Morocco. These were two very different cultural groups, different from each other and quite different from the average Israeli citizen of those times.

"The eastern, or Asian, Jew—while remaining very Jewish, in terms of religion, study of the ancient texts, traditions —had assimilated many of the Arab cultural patterns. He was inclined to have many children, as an economic guarantee for his old age.

"Arab society is a patriarchal society, with authority and commitment flowing from parents down to children. I mean the parents were more important than the children, and everything had to be done for the convenience of the parents. Girls were trained to help the mother and take over many of the household chores. Boys were sent out to work young and bring the money back to the father. This was the very opposite of European traditions in Israel, where the Jewish child is a jewel, a family treasure, and the parents sacrifice everything to give the child the best chance for life.

"The North African Jew was again different. He had been assimilated by deliberate French colonial policy. He did not know Hebrew, or very little. His culture was provincial French. Where the Asian Jew had in many instances absorbed Arab culture and enjoyed a rather close Semitic co-

existence with Arabs, the North African Jew was more likely
to have allied himself with the French, as the superior culture, and to look down upon the Arab.

"Neither the Asian Jew nor the African Jew was prepared
for the European culture of Israel. The cultural shock was
tremendous. No one was really prepared for it, and even when
it became apparent, it was denied for too long.

"Ben-Gurion and other leaders could not bring themselves
to admit such great differences among Jews. When complaints
came in from teachers that many of their students were not
learning and could not learn under existing curricula and
methods, they were told to try harder, to give extra time for
make-up work after school. But by the middle and late fifties
the tragic truth could no longer be denied. Only forty percent
of the children could read with any degree of fluency after
five and more years of schooling! In a free Jewish state!

"The government panicked and hastily called in educators
for a crash replanning of the system. A special department
was created to plan help for disadvantaged children and backward children. It hurt so much to think that Jewish children
could be backward or disadvantaged that when they set up
their new schools for them, they called them 'schools in need
of development' instead of schools for children in need of
development.

"This was quite right. Why brand the child if the system
is at fault? I am proud of our government's feeling of shame.
It is all to the credit of Israel. And it shows how ridiculous
are the charges of discrimination. Mistakes we made. Discrimination, never."

Professor Minkowich sighed and rubbed his forehead.

"Well, we are on the right track now. But it is still a difficult, slow process. Boys and girls have been increasingly integrated in studies and pace of studies. Special remedial help
has cut down the gap. Our methods are constantly improving
and in time education will wipe out achievement differences,

except for those real differences among human beings independent of other factors.

"But those other factors are still a block to the creation of truly equal status for all citizens. The best schools cannot fully compensate for crowded homes. Housing is a key element of the educational process, although it is not often thought of as such. A balanced diet, essential to physical health, is also important for mental health. A tired, ill-nourished child cannot be a good student.

"We have a long way to go. But let no one say that we are not straining every effort. Israel is a young nation, with crushing military obligations on the budget and on manpower. We can do a lot better but we are doing the best we can right now."

\* \* \*

While I was talking with government officials, editors, and university professors about the Ashkenazic-Sephardic problem, co-authors Robert and Lucy Szekely were out talking with their own age group and meeting with the Black Panthers. The following is their report:

We were told that the Pantherim have a favorite hangout, a coffeehouse called Ta'amon, on the corner of King George and Hillel, on a wide square not far from the King David Hotel in central Jerusalem.

Before going there, we had first walked through the streets of the Musrara slums to get "a feel" of the place where they lived. We are familiar with the slum areas of New York, particularly the East Village—we lived in the West Village, on Bank Street—and we expected to see familiar slum sights.

The slums of Jerusalem were not at all like the slums of New York. The buildings were weather-stained and cracked. The streets were more turd-lined than tree-lined, and by Jerusalem standards it was clearly a slum district. But not by New York standards. For one thing, there is the sunlight of Jerusalem which laves the streets and buildings as the sun does not do in New York. The sun turns New York into a furnace in summer and its glaring light exposes the ugly, soot-streaked face of the New York slums.

We called on people we had met in coffeehouses and cafés. Their apartments were small, smelling of food and washing and the bitter, acrid odors of poverty. One couple we called on had no chairs. We all sat on beds or mattresses on the floor. But we saw no evidence and heard no complaints about muggings, dope addicts, rapists, and all the plagues of New York's slums.

We do not mean to make invidious comparisons. New York is too easy a target to shoot at for the sake of shooting. We think the comparison is useful for American readers to get some idea of what is meant by the word "slum" when used in a different country. By Israeli standards, the slums of Jerusalem and Tel Aviv are, indeed, slums. On an American scale, they are substandard districts, seriously overcrowded, with inadequate plumbing, but not anything like an American big-city slum.

We made our way to the Ta'amon café to find the Panthers, thinking it interesting that their meeting place was not in their own neighborhood. In America, groups, movements, gangs normally stay on their own "turf," but not in Israel. We wondered if perhaps they were not so alienated from the dominant Ashkenazim as we had heard.

The Ta'amon coffeehouse looks like a subway train, long, narrow, with tables lined up, one next to the other, on the length of each wall. Each table serves six people and there is no such thing as privacy. You come in and sit down at whatever available space there is, with whoever is already seated at the table.

We heard a mixed chorus of Hebrew and French from the tables on the left as we entered, and realized that this was the Moroccan contingent. We could not find two free places together there and were conscious of a noticeable lack of welcome, so we turned to the tables on the right. There were free places there and the languages were Hebrew and English. It only took a few minutes to find out the differences between the two ranks of tables: on the left were the Panthers and on the right were the Panther-watchers, a gaggle of university students, sociologists, and reporters all studying the Panthers and preparing articles or theses on them. One of them, Saul Neumann, told us, "You know, I think there are more Panther-watchers than Panthers."

There were, we were told, no accurate statistics on the membership of the Panther movement. Estimates ran from 1,500 to 7,000, although the higher figure was not credited by many. The Panther leaders refuse to give any figures. Even those sociology students most sympathetic to the cause believe the lower figure more likely correct.

As we talked and watched, we suddenly heard shouting and noise in the street just outside the café. Two slim, short young men were fighting. One of the observers said, "That's Saadi Marciano, leader of the Panthers. I don't know the other one."

No one had moved to stop the fight when suddenly a Mustang, driving by, braked with a screech of tires. A big, beefy man, well over six feet tall and two hundred and fifty pounds, came jumping out. He ran over to the fighting boys, grabbed each by the neck, and picked them off their feet, like a giant bear plucking chickens out of a coop, while bellowing, in English, "Now, cut it out! Break it up, break it up!"

None of the Panthers, and neither of the fighters, could speak English, but they understood what he was saying and doing. The onlookers gathered around him and shouted at him in mixed French and Hebrew to let the boys alone. He finally put them down and said, "Don't we Jews have enough enemies without fighting among ourselves?"

Someone translated his words. Marciano grinned and said, in French, "I've got a lot of enemies." But he offered his hand to the American, and with motions invited him in for a cup of coffee. The American, a tourist who had just happened to be passing by, shook hands and said his wife was waiting for him and he had to go on. As he left, he delivered a farewell word of advice, "We can't afford to fight each other. Now, you guys knock it off."

Marciano and the young man he had been fighting came into the café together and joined their friends, making sarcastic remarks about American Jews who thought they owned Israel. One hears a lot of grumbling about Americans in Israel, and it disturbs many American visitors who come with shining eyes and open hearts, hands, and pocketbooks and are surprised at something less than a hearty welcome.

Not that the majority of Israelis are not keenly conscious of the vital nature of American support, without which Israel could not have survived. And not that they are ungrateful or resentful. By and large, relations are good. But the proprietary air and thousand-percent "patriotism" of some American visitors irritate a number of Israelis and particularly those like the Panthers who do not think that Israel is the land of milk and honey and justice, at least not for them.

By then we had introduced ourselves to the Panther tables, and since we spoke fluent French and did not mention we were American reporters, they asked us to sit down and have a coffee with them.

They wanted to know all about the student uprisings in Paris—in 1968—and what had happened since. The ones we met that day were all Moroccans and wanted to know if we had been to Morocco. We had, and knew it well, and it helped break down the barriers between us. Not that they had any love for Morocco or any sympathy for France. On the contrary, they were bitter, as all Israelis are, at the French "betrayal" of Israel and the sale of arms to the Arabs.

A few of them mentioned that they were going to Tel Aviv for the weekend. We invited them to a buffet dinner at our apartment and they agreed to come. We then told them that we were writing a book about young Israelis and wondered whether they would agree to be interviewed and quoted. After some discussion and hesitation, they agreed.

They came, with their friend and adviser, Naomi Kies.

Miss Kies was born and raised in the Bronx and Yonkers, New York. She did her undergraduate work at Swarthmore and then took her Ph.D. in sociology at M.I.T. in 1970, writing her doctoral dissertation on the election results in Jerusalem. She lived and researched in Jerusalem from 1967 until she finished her doctoral work, and then immigrated to Israel, where she became a citizen in 1971.

With her were three Panthers: Elie Abekser, Shalom "Charlie" Bitton (the most vocal of them, a leader of the group), and Kochavi Shemesh. Kochavi was born in Baghdad in 1944 and came to Israel at the age of six. Charlie was born in Casablanca in 1947 and came to Israel with his parents in 1949. Elie was born in Casablanca in 1949, was raised there, and only came to Israel at fifteen, alone, to visit with cousins. In 1965, he applied for immigration and citizenship.

At first, they were all shy and resentful. Our apartment in Tel Aviv was a comfortable but modest little place, in our eyes. It was a fifth-floor walk-up: one long room, divided by a curtain into a living room and bedroom alcove, with a small terrace, on the street, a tiny kitchenette, toilet and small bathroom. But to the Panthers it was a luxury flat and categorized us as rich—the other half, the enemy.

Our buffet spread was also modest—cold meats, cold vegetables, lots of peppers, sour cream, rye bread and the flat Arab bread (a favorite in Israel), one bottle of whisky, a bottle of wine, and a lot of soda pop and Seltzer water. But the Panthers stalked around the table taking almost nothing, perhaps more ill-at-ease than hostile.

Naomi Kies stepped gracefully into the breach, began a conversation with us about America, the social conflicts there, the youth movement, the war in Vietnam, and gradually, skillfully, drew her Panther friends into the general discussion.

Some of the comments surprised us.

Elie Abekser, listening intently to a discussion of the social welfare issue, suddenly interjected, "Social welfare is no good. We don't want charity, no handouts. We want our due: a decent place to live, jobs, equal status."

He also showed no sympathy with American youth protests about the war in Vietnam. "America is right to stop the communists. The Vietnamese, the North African Arab revolutionaries—they do not care about people. I fought Arabs in the streets of Casablanca. That's one reason I came here; I couldn't live there."

Elie is having trouble with the immigration authorities, a rare case in Israel, where immigration procedures are very efficient and simple for any Jew who seeks to become an Israeli. He applied for immigration after having lived three years with his cousins. He had, however, neglected to file his papers properly and in time to get the special privileges accorded to an immigrant during the first three years of residence under immigrant status. He claimed the three-year privilege after the three-year period had gone by without proper registration.

The authorities granted him citizenship and gave him his Israeli passport and papers, but said that they could not retroactively grant him the special new-immigrant allowances. Elie conceded, "They offered me money. But I don't want money, I want my rights."

He admitted he was offered full and immediate citizenship, plus a financial grant to help him out. He acknowledged he had been negligent in following procedures. He argued that the officials should have overlooked bureaucratic rules and given him the three-year status he wanted. He felt that this was discrimination.

*        *        *

Shalom "Charlie" Bitton, unlike Elie, was almost a native-born Israeli, being a baby of two when his parents immigrated. He was one of the first citizens of the new state. He went through eight years of elementary school and two years of vocational school, learning the well-paid and much-needed craft of machine tooling.

"We had a hard time of it," said Charlie. "At first, my father and mother could not find a house or an apartment. They pitched a tent and lived in a field. Then we got a very small apartment. But the babies were coming—there are six of us kids in the family. We had to share a kitchen and a stand-up toilet with other families.

"My father got word from a friend one day that some houses had been vacated in 'no man's land'—the sector in Jerusalem between the Israeli and the Jordanian army lines. My father ran over, picked out one of the empty houses, and called us to move our furniture and clothes over. No one wanted it; we took it. That was early in 1950. I have only the vaguest memories—I was only three—but my father told me all about it.

"The water was cut off, the lights were cut off. There was occasional sniper firing back and forth. It was a hell of a way to live."

We asked Charlie why his father had not tried to get a better apartment than the one they had abandoned for the house between the hostile lines of fire. We wanted to know whether he had applied for a home loan, what work his father did. We received evasive answers.

Charlie is on the police books. He was jailed for burglary. He is not a hardened criminal by any standard. He is weak, sulky, self-pitying to some extent. One can sympathize up to a point with his plight and his difficult early childhood and life. But, as in the case of Elie, he did not present a strong case against Israeli society or the government.

Charlie received a good education: ten years of general and technical training. He had been prepared by the state to cope with life. Machine-tool workers are not unemployed in Israel. To try to draw any kind of analogy between Charlie Bitton and an American Black Panther is just so much nonsense. This is not to say that Israel does not have a social problem. It does. But young men like Charlie Bitton are not typical of or the most convincing spokesmen for the issue.

\* \* \*

Kochavi Shemesh, the Iraqi-born Black Panther, came to Israel with his mother and a younger brother when he was six years old. They spent one night, he said, in a transit camp in Haifa and then went on to Jerusalem, where his father had found lodging in the back of a store. It was in the sector near the front lines that cut through Jerusalem. Dayan had ordered fences and barriers and some houses torn down to clear a line of fire and set up observation posts. The police cleared the area and told the family to move into the Musrara sector.

Officials took them to a small apartment that was available, but, said Kochavi, "My father said the rooms were too small. Besides, he did not have the money to make a down payment to buy the apartment. We were too poor."

We asked why they had not been offered home-loan aids, as other immigrants had been given.

"Oh, well, he could have gotten help. But my father did not want to carry a mortgage and have it hanging on his neck for years."

The more they talked, the less convincing their cases seemed. These were not victims of an evil or even an inefficient social system. These unfortunate men were dropouts, from families that could not or would not try to make it. Their lives would not have been easy even if they had more stamina and character. There are inequities in the Israeli system. But inequities, failures, do not add up to a charge of deliberate discrimination, and certainly not racial discrimination.

Kochavi told us he was not working. Then he added, "Well, I'm working full-time for the Panthers."

When we asked if he had ever been employed, he said bitterly, "Sure, I worked and wanted to work but they wouldn't let me. They just threw me out, although I did my job all right."

We asked who "they" were and why he thought they had thrown him out of whatever he was doing.

His face darkened, his lips twisted, and his black eyes burned with anger.

"I'll tell you the story. Maybe then you'll understand what happens here.

"My mother got a job as a cleaning woman in one of the institutions run by Hadassah. One day, she spoke to a scientist whose laboratory she was cleaning. She told him she had a son who wanted to work, but had to get a job which did not require great strength, because I had polio as a kid. She begged him to find me something.

"He was a nice guy. He called me in, talked to me, and offered to train me as a lab assistant. It was a government job—not much, of course; I was only a kid, about sixteen. But it was a job, gave us some money. I was very happy and said I would do everything to be a good assistant.

"It worked out pretty well and everything was going fine. Then, one day, a government investigator came by and found me on the payroll doing this work. He questioned me about my education and training, and then he told me that I did not have the necessary credits and qualifications to hold down the job I had been given. So they threw me out. Okay, so now I work for the Panther organization."

We asked Charlie, the best-qualified of the leaders, if he was working or planned to find employment. He muttered, "No, I have a personal problem."

Elie told us he was not working, either.

"I was in an automobile accident. I injured my arm and

I can't do heavy work. I did get a job as a night watchman, but they found out I had a jail record and was not qualified to carry a gun. So I lost the job.

"What was I jailed for? Oh, I had a row with a girl friend and I beat her up."

(We checked later and discovered that the girl, an Arab, a minor under sixteen, had been severely beaten and that Elie had been sentenced to two years in jail for violent assault and corrupting a minor.)

We served coffee and then they left. We were sure we would not hear much about them, for they were not leaders and theirs was not a dynamic movement. One year has gone by from our meeting with the Panthers and the completion of this text. They have not been heard from in this year. They were, in retrospect, a mass-media phenomenon.

We were also sure, and became more certain in months of investigation, that the problem of the socially disadvantaged was a real one, that the economic and cultural differences between Afro-Asian- and European-origin Jews were wide and would grow greater unless major long-term programs were instituted. Finally, interviews with government officials and those of private social welfare agencies indicated that they were aware of the seriousness of the problem, were taking steps to solve it, with a growing public concern behind them.

Robert Szekely, an economist and analyst, concluded that the Ashkenazic-Sephardic social strains would last a long time, even given the government's good will and the many public expressions of concern.

"Good will is not enough," Robert wrote in his report on the issue. "Even money is not enough, for the processes of education are slow and the gap is wide. It is the Arab danger from outside that helps maintain the internal cohesion of Israel and plaster over the gaps. The disadvantaged Afro-Asian Jews are largely anti-Arab and highly patriotic. This is a saving factor of great importance."

We checked the findings of our interviews on this issue against the figures of the Continuing Survey, which explored two questions in this area in October-December, 1971. The following are their findings:

CONTINUING SURVEY:
QUESTION B1—Transfer of a part of the defense budget to the social welfare budget

Some believe that in present circumstances the government should transfer funds from the defense budget (without endangering the purchase of military equipment) to the budgets for housing, social services, and aid to the most disadvantaged sectors of the population; others argue that this is not the time to effect such a transfer. What is your opinion?

|  | Youth % | Adults % |
|---|---|---|
| It is absolutely necessary to transfer funds from the defense budget to the budgets for housing and social aid | 25 | 13 |
| Perhaps such a transfer should be carried out | 33 | 21 |
| Perhaps such a transfer should not be carried out | 12 | 13 |
| We must not make such a transfer | 30 | 53 |
|  | 100 | 100 |

The figures are eloquent testimony to the social conscience of the new—the first—generation of Israeli citizens.

One should recall the context of this question. It is not a relatively clear issue of providing more social welfare funds but of doing so at the expense of the military in a situation where the country is surrounded by enemies against whom citizens fought three wars. It is the young people who would be putting their lives into the front line if war were to break out again, yet it is that young combat generation which is ready to take the risk of cutting the defense budget for social welfare progress. This augurs well for the future solution of the problem.

The optimism, of young and old both, expressed itself in answers to a question on relations between the two Jewish communities:

CONTINUING SURVEY:
QUESTION B2—Intercommunity relations

There exist several communities in Israel, such as the Ashkenazim and the Sephardim. In your opinion, are relations between those communities good at the present time?

|  | Youth % | Adults % |
|---|---|---|
| Very good | 4 | 5 |
| Good enough | 37 | 43 |
| Not very good | 46 | 41 |
| Not good at all | 13 | 11 |
|  | 100 | 100 |

More than eight out of ten Israelis, both youth and adults, think that relations between Jews of different cultural origins are good enough or partially good. This could mean, of course, that they are closing their eyes to the truth. But they are not, as our own two hundred in-depth interviews over a broad spectrum of the population revealed to us. The opinion that there was a serious problem was almost unanimous. The national poll thus reflects the views of a people who recognize a grave problem but are confident that they can solve it.

# X

# The New Israelis
# and Judaism

For he established a testimony in Jacob,
and appointed a law in Israel, which he commanded our fathers, that they should make
them known to their children: that the generation to come might know them, even the children which should be born. . . .

—PSALM 78:5–6.

No problem excites Jews more than the problem of the Jewish religion, except possibly the one question on which there is no general agreement at all: What is a Jew?

We soon stopped asking "What is a Jew?" because of the variety and complexity of answers we received. But we did ask and did receive clear although surprising answers to the question we put to each of the two hundred interviewees: How religious are you; to what extent do you observe religious ritual?

What follows is a report of the replies and a compilation of the percentages, including the results of two national surveys.

*   *   *

We met Lea and Yussef through Johnny Eytan, son of Walter Eytan, distinguished Israeli diplomat, long-time Ambassador to Paris.

Johnny works for an insurance company. Lea, age twenty-one, is studying and teaching political science at the Hebrew University. Her husband, Yussef, twenty-four years old, is a scholar of Hebrew, a "Yeshiva *buche,*" who lives for and in the ancient texts, from five in the morning until late at night.

"Mine is an old, old native family," said Yussef, rubbing his short black beard. "We have lived in Jerusalem for a century and more." He paused and laughed, "I should explain —that is, my mother's family is of this soil. My father was born in Lithuania.

"We believe in religion and tradition. It is very important to us. I feel a personal kinship with thousands of years of history of a great people. However, I see no reason to impose what I believe and what I feel on everybody else.

"Of course, there must be respect for the sensitivities of the religious by those who do not share our deep faith. They should not violate our Sabbath, our prayers, the principles of our education. The religious and nonreligious communities should make every effort to coexist or Israel could be rent asunder. Tolerance is the great virtue, the goal—mutual tolerance."

"Yussi is right," said his wife, Lea.

"Those of us who wish to maintain a religious way of life should do so, but without trying to make everyone do as we do. I am against the Religious Party. Society must not be ruled by religious factions."

Both Lea and Yussef agreed that the religious question is a vexing one and that relations between the religious and nonreligious communities are not good. But they were not pessimistic about the future. "There is a very militant but minority religious faction among the young, those who stone people who ride on the Sabbath. They shouldn't stone people, of course, but then it is rude to flaunt the Sabbath in the neighborhood of those who are devout.

"But these are exceptions. Most young people are more tolerant, more sensitive than the extreme cases that make the headlines and get talked about. The ranks of the orthodox are thinning among the young generation. Maybe that is why the minority, feeling threatened, becomes more militant."

Lea warned us not to make the mistake of thinking that Jewishness is diminishing along with orthodoxy. "We are Jews here in Israel. We are proud of our heritage. There is no diminution of faith and culture among our new generation. But some of us have different ways of being Jewish.

"Some think Jewish culture is more important than the rituals of the religion. Now, that can be dangerous in a big, powerful, assimilating society like America's. If Jews in America move away from their religion, they might find out one day that their children are not Jews any more. But this is Israel, a Jewish state. We are so secure in our Jewishness that we do not have to be as strict in our observance.

"I am not talking about myself, for we are religious, but I can understand and not hate those who are not. And we do not believe in religious laws applied by the state. You can't tell people how to feel. You can't legislate faith."

We said earlier in this report that it is difficult to generalize about Israelis, for they are a highly civilized, thus complex people. In the course of our interviews, we would almost always find a moment when we had reached a conclusion about the interviewee's political orientation and then hear an answer inconsistent with what had been said before.

Lea and Yussef had seemed to us fairly conservative young people. Neither was an activist in politics. Their views on freedom of religion were liberal, but their general views, life style, and somewhat self-satisfied pronouncements seemed, at the very least, moderate. Yet when we asked about Vietnam, they said, "It's a failure, a big mistake."

Many Israelis and most conservatives support America, believe that America has been fighting communism in Southeast Asia. They see Russian presence in the Middle East as linked with the communist move "to take over Asia." Golda Meir has privately and publicly endorsed American efforts, perhaps because she is so dependent upon American aid that she cannot afford any kind of friction on an issue so important to Washington.

But Lea said, "Vietnam does not affect our vital interests, and the sooner America is free of that burden the better." And Yussef added, "With or without Vietnam, America has enough resources to help us and cannot let Russia or communists take over the Middle East. You ought to get out of Vietnam for your own good. It's a cancer for America."

Yussef felt that one of the problems of America is that "almost every American has his family and ancestral roots in some other country. Here, all of us Israelis have our roots not only in a country but in a religion and a culture: Judaism. That is the importance of religion in our society.

"If Israelis were to drift away from religion, if Israel were to become just another nationalist state, then there would be no justification for having a state of Israel. The fact that it is a Jewish state, a homeland for people so long persecuted, living under the laws of another group—this is meaningful, this justifies the sacrifices, this gives true justification for having created Israel here in Palestine. But if we are not going to be Jewish, then by what right are we here and why is the state needed?"

We asked him if there were not some kind of contradiction between his view that Israel must be a Jewish state and Israelis must be religious rather than merely nationalist and his earlier view that the state and the religious factions should not impose religious laws.

"No, it is not a contradiction; it is a dilemma," replied Yussef. "Imposition of religion is impossible. As Lea said, 'You can't legislate faith.' It would be undemocratic—fascist, in fact—to become legally a theocratic state. We cannot, must not, do this. But if, in freedom, people lose faith and abandon religion, then all will be lost. This is our challenge. We must keep the faith freely and voluntarily if we want to keep Israel for what it is meant to be."

Lea and Yussef live in Jerusalem, where there is a strong, militant religious community in frequent conflict with the less formally devout Jews. Many religious Jews sought peace and unity in religious communities, such as the "religious kibbutz" Yavne.

Kibbutz Yavne was founded by devout and socialist Jews who wanted to live in a community of their own. But, as has happened in almost all the kibbutzim over the years, the original aims have been altered, new thoughts and customs evolved, and, although it is still essentially a kibbutz of people who profess and practice religion and socialist ideas, a number of changes have been instituted by the new generation.

In the early days, all the moneys earned by the kibbutz

belonged to the kibbutz as a collective, and not to the original members. Houses were built and furnished according to a plan, and everyone received not only equal shares but identical shares; that is, the same kind of curtains, the same radio set, etc.

Today everyone gets the same allotment, but it is given in cash, and each member can spend his cash to buy what he wants for himself, not according to a master plan. Attendance at prayers and religious ceremonies is expected and encouraged but not obligatory. In what was once a bastion of religious influence, religion, while still dominant, is not a controlling element.

\*      \*      \*

We called upon a young married couple, Eli and Yaffa, and their three young children, at Kibbutz Yavne.

Their living quarters in no way resemble the log-cabin image of the kibbutz. It looks more like a college dormitory in an American university, although considerably neater and more middle-class.

It is a one-room flat, about seventeen feet long by twelve feet wide, extended by a balcony facing a tree-lined street in the kibbutz. The balcony, six feet by nine, is big enough to dine on or to relax on with drinks and friends in the golden evening sun that gives a soft line and radiance to the stark, geometrical, undecorated stucco buildings.

Outside of Jerusalem, Israeli communities are not pleasant to look upon. There is a natural beauty and the patina of antiquity in the hills of Haifa, the verdant lands of Galilee, the brilliantly kaleidoscopic semiwilderness of the Negev, but what man has built in Israel is often hastily thrown up for utilitarian purposes.

Eli and Yaffa have done the best they could to turn their one-room-kitchenette-bathroom flat into comfortable living quarters for a family of five. They have a radio, a refrigerator, a portable grill and hot plate, bookshelves lined with books (some two hundred crowded from floor to ceiling). They have saved space by using a daytime sofa that converts into a nighttime double bed, and folding cots for the children.

The room is carpeted, furnished simply with a table and five chairs. In the kitchenette there is Pyrex kitchenware from France. There is a small liquor cabinet. ("We don't drink, ourselves; it's for guests," they told us.) The walls are decorated with modern paintings. (Israel has a new crop of promising young artists. Jews have not, in the past, been prominent in painting—Chagall and a few others excepted.)

Eli and Yaffa sometimes take snacks in the kitchenette or on the balcony, but most of the meals are eaten in the communal dining room of the kibbutz. In the early days, everyone ate in the communal dining room, but today members have the option of cooking in their own quarters and the kibbutz gives them a food allowance if they so choose. The food allowance is drawn from the communal kitchen on the morning of the day the member chooses to eat at home. This was once regarded as antisocial, but the young generation needs and demands a certain measure of privacy and family life.

Eli came to Kibbutz Yavne with his father and mother when he was two years old. He is twenty-seven. Thus, almost all of his life he has been a kibbutznik, living in a religious kibbutz. But, he says, "I am not the model of a religious man. There are too many rules and regulations for me. I am religious in my own way. Not ritually."

Eli's father is a highly educated, skilled man, who took his doctorate in chemistry in Italy and worked as a researcher and part owner of a pharmaceutical firm there. Eli's mother is a musician, a teacher of piano and harmony. Both are highly idealistic and came to Israel just before World War II to take up life in a kibbutz, not as refugees, not to seek security, for they were successful members of Italian society, but to satisfy an inner drive for a more idealistic life.

Eli studied chemistry, like his father, but took a technical certificate rather than an advanced academic degree.

"I wanted to know what I needed to know to make a success of my assignment in the kibbutz. I felt no urge to take my doctorate or even my bachelor's. I am working on the manufacture and packaging of foodstuffs."

The differences between Eli and his father are typical of the main differences between the old and new generations of Israel. The old: idealistic, socialistic, radical in ideas and life style, adventurous and pioneering. The new: materialistic, pragmatic, moderate or conservative in life style, devoted to Israel and Judaism but not devout about their devotion.

Eli's wife, Yaffa, came to the kibbutz when she was twelve years old, and she is now twenty-five. She came alone, sent there by parents who wanted her to be raised in a kibbutz, although they themselves did not feel qualified for kibbutz life. One encounters this phenomenon often enough. It is something like Irish parents sending their daughter to be brought up in a convent.

Yaffa met Eli at the kibbutz, where she works as a teacher and administrative official. She took her B.A. in Hebrew and philosophy at the university.

"Religion is a matter of conscience," she said, "and I think most Israelis are, in their conscience, Jews, whether they practice all the rituals correctly or consistently or not. The religious problem will work itself out in the long run. It is not really a religious problem. It is essentially a political problem, a fight for the soul of Israel between those who think you cannot be a good Jew, or have a healthy Israel, without strict devotions and those who think you can.

"Politico-religious quarrels can be very grave, as we see in Ireland, for example, but that is not the case of Israel. The differences between orthodox, conservative, reformed, and nonpracticing Jews are not so fundamental, so grave, as religious quarrels between Catholics and Protestants, particularly, as in the case of Ireland, when nationalist politics is at the core of the conflict between religious factions. We'll solve it, believe me, we'll solve it."

Whatever issue we touched upon, whatever problem was invoked in Israel we constantly found a willingness to concede the problem, even to admit it was serious, but always those last words, "We'll solve it"—a deep-rooted optimism, or, perhaps, self-assurance. It is one of the most admirable, enviable, and endearing qualities of the Israelis. It more than compensates for some of their less endearing qualities: smugness to the point of arrogance, a teasing "put-down" way of debating, and the barb thrown at every visitor: "If you're so interested in Israel, why don't you come and live here?"

Yaffa is more political than Eli, although not an activist in politics—we found very few young Israelis politically active. Army service from eighteen to twenty-one, then the full efforts required to find a job, a career, to start a family generally delay political activities until the thirties.

"I voted the Poali Mizrachi ticket," said Yaffa. "That's one of the religious parties, but perhaps less militant about religious laws than the other religious parties. I think it is more Zionist in orientation.

"Why did I vote for them? Well, I admit I don't identify completely with them, but I think the religious influence is important—it should not die out—and I didn't like the other parties, the secular parties.

"This nation must become one and must be a Jewish nation. At the same time, I think State and Church should be separate; that is, have separate domains, secular law and religious law. I know it's complicated and sounds contradictory. It's hard to explain. We must be a nation of Jews but not a theocratic state. We must find this line.

"And then there is Zionism, the principle that all Jews live in the Jewish homeland. This, too, gets complicated. Some think it means all Jews should be able to live in Zion;

some think all Jews must live in Zion."

We laughed and asked her if she knew the joke current in the American Jewish community: A Zionist is a New York Jew who works selflessly and tirelessly to send other Jews to Israel.

She said she had not heard that but that she had been told that when two Jews meet in America, they argue about how much a third Jew should contribute to the aid-for-Israel campaign.

"It is truly wonderful what American Jews do to help Israel," she said. Then, with typical Israeli arrogant humor, she added, "But what better could they do with their money? We are the ultimate defenders of Judaism and the Jews in the world.

"We make sacrifices, too, for our fellow-Jews. We have opened the gates of Israel to all Jews who seek refuge or a Jewish life in the homeland. In fact, we now do more for the *olim,* the immigrants, than we do for the sabras. That is the principal complaint of people like the Black Panthers.

"It is true that new immigrants, particularly now those who come from Russia, get more help and much better new housing than the Sephardim who came from the Middle East or North Africa in the fifties. Many of them are living in the jerry-built flats built twenty years ago, which are now slums and hovels, whereas new immigrants get the best modern flats.

"This is not fair. The tactics of the Black Panthers are very irritating and they are not admirable people, but there has been an injustice done and it must be corrected, even at the expense of spending less on defense and more on social problems.

"This is one of the things I don't like about the religious parties, even though I vote for one of them. They worry more about how food is made kosher, or about marriage and divorce laws, than they do about how people are living. Religious leaders care less about reality than about what is written in the Scriptures. They would have us live the way Jews lived thousands of years ago. That is not possible.

"They don't think that women should serve in the army. They want us to sit separately from the men in *shul* and pray separately at the Wall. Are we really 'unclean vessels'? That is infuriating. I served in the army; I was an officer, although I could have had a religious exemption. I am religious but I want no exemption, no special privileges or denial of rights."

We asked about women's rights in the kibbutz.

Yaffa smiled and said, "We have all the equal rights. We can work like the men and with the men. Of course, we do most of the housework and cooking—woman's work, I guess, although the most famous cooks in the world are men.

"There is the one thing men cannot do, carry a child in a womb. Yes, that is our work. And we all have many children—three, four, five. The kibbutz needs children, the state needs children; Israel has a small population. But, more than that, we want children, not just as a duty. They are our joy."

Yaffa laughed. "The worst time for a woman in the kibbutz is the first year of marriage when she is waiting, praying to be pregnant. It is terrifying to be a young bride—surrounded by women with swollen stomachs, with a kid on each hip— and walk around slim. It's worse than being naked in a crowd. But it doesn't last long. We are a fertile people. Look around our kibbutz, you will see the future of Israel.

"As for religion, who knows where the pendulum will swing? Our parents were very religious, socialistic, radical. We are less religious, materialistic, liberal. Maybe our kids will be more like their grandparents, maybe not. Be sure, however, that there will be an Israel and it will be a Jewish state, however its people interpret or practice Judaism. We have not fought our way back from two thousand years of exile to give up everything we stand for."

\*    \*    \*

Not all religious Israelis are so reasonable and tolerant as Lea and Yussef, Eli and Yaffa. Many of the ultraorthodox and most of the Hasidim, easily recognized by their round black hats, full beards, flowing sideburns, and long black coats, are quick to stone or spit at any real or imagined violation of their code. They consider even rabbis to be sinners if they represent reformed or conservative sects. Orthodoxy alone is tolerated by the orthodox.

Only one of ten of the new Israeli generation considers himself a totally observant Jew, as the Continuing Survey informed us, and even of those, according to our own interviews, only about half, barely 5%, could be described as inflexibly and intolerantly orthodox.

There is one subgroup among the very religious that is particularly interesting and that plays a role far greater than its numbers would suggest. These are the religious Zionists, many of them immigrants, particularly from the orthodox communities of America. They are both deeply religious and militantly nationalistic. It is they who were among the first to volunteer for the founding of new settlements in frontier regions. It is they who resist any talk of returning the occupied territories to the Arabs. They believe in Eretz Israel—a Greater Israel, encompassing all the lands on which Jews lived in Biblical times.

A striking example of this kind of "new Israelite"—in some ways an atavism to fanatical sects of antiquity—can be found in Hebron, reclaimed from Jordan after the Six-Day War, or in some of the new settlements in the Gaza Strip, where future negotiations are being heavily mortgaged by the creation of new "facts"; that is, the encrustation of new Jewish communities which future governments will find hard to abandon.

The ancient and modern histories of Hebron illustrate dramatically the nature of the problem any negotiator faces when trying to solve the dispute over the frontiers of Israel and its Arab neighbors. It is a vexing, even agonizing problem for young Israelis, who are forced to defend, and may have to stake their lives one day to hold, territories whose fate has been decided in some instances by a very small minority of their fellows.

Fervent Zionists who lay claim to Hebron base that claim on a long history of Jewish occupation of Hebron.

Four thousand years ago, Abraham paid four hundred shekels of silver for a field containing a cave where he buried his wife, and where he, his son, and his grandson were also buried. Abraham's family burial place still exists in Hebron today as a revered shrine, known as the Tomb of the Patriarchs.

Three thousand years ago, David was proclaimed king in Hebron, and the city remained his royal seat until he captured Jerusalem, seven years later.

In 1268, the Mameluke rulers of Hebron forbade the Jews entrance into the Tomb of the Patriarchs. They were allowed only to pray on the steps, up to the thirteenth step. This Mameluke decree of the mid-thirteenth century remained in effect and practice in Hebron right through its capture by the Jews in 1967.

In 1540, ten Jewish families, led by Rabbi Makiel Ashkenazi of Venice, purchased a small square of land from the Karaites of Hebron. This area became the "ghetto" of Hebron. Rabbi Makiel brought with him the process for manufacturing colored Venetian glass, still used today and known as Hebron glass.

All during this long period of history, Jews were living in Hebron. Indeed, from the time of the return from the Babylonian exile, in the sixth century B.C., to the massacre of the Jews in 1929, Jewish settlement in Hebron was uninterrupted.

The massacre took place in 1929 in tragic circumstances alas only too familiar to students of Jewish history. Jews were living peacefully with Arabs in Hebron—more than peacefully, for relations between the two communities were excellent. But there was conflict not far away in Jerusalem. (Hebron is roughly equidistant between Jerusalem and Beersheba.) The Jews in Hebron were so confident of their good relations with their Moslem neighbors that, despite the rioting in Jerusalem, they refused the offer of a self-defense unit which the Hagana (the Jewish Defense Force) was prepared to send to Hebron.

A number of Hebronite Arabs went to Jerusalem to join the Arab forces fighting there. Some of them were killed in the battles that raged through Jerusalem. Their friends returned to Hebron and reported that the Jews had slaughtered Hebronites who had gone to Jerusalem. The Arabs, an unstable and easily inflamed group, formed quickly into angry mobs and went from house to house searching out Jews for vengeance. By dawn, sixty-six Jews had been massacred, all of them defenseless because they had refused to defend themselves, all of them friendly to the Arabs who slaughtered them.

It should also be recorded, so that the truth be known and honorable Arabs be honored as they merit, that some four hundred Jews were saved by twenty-eight Arab families who rushed to warn them of the peril and who hid them in their own homes.

Not all Arabs are mad with blood lust; not all Arabs are unstable and inflammable. The trouble is that too many of them are unstable and inflammable for any Jews to live among them without the strongest possible defense forces. It is such historical memories as the massacre of Hebron which make peace negotiations so difficult in the Middle East, to say nothing of the deep-rooted anxieties of Jews anywhere and everywhere.

All the Jews left Hebron after the tragedy of 1929. But Jews yearn for their ancestral homes. Some Jews returned to Germany after the Hitler holocaust, and some Jews returned to Hebron in 1931, only two years after the massacre. But they found no peace or friendship left in Hebron. Even their old friends, fearful of a new incident, begged them to leave. They did, in 1936. Their homes were taken by the Arabs, their shrines desecrated. Their four-century-old synagogue was leveled and a public latrine erected on its site.

In 1968, a year after the city had been captured in the Six-Day War, Rabbi Moshe Levinger, a former Yeshiva teacher and kibbutznik, led a group of fellow-Jews in a campaign to force the government to permit the establishment of a Jewish settlement in Hebron. There were no Jews there, only Arabs, but, as the rabbi argued, "There are no Jews in Hebron, not because it is not a Jewish city but because the Arabs drove us out. We have a right to return."

When no positive action was taken by the government, Rabbi Levinger and his friends decided to "create facts." On Passover Eve, 1968, a group of eighty Jews moved into the Park Hotel on the outskirts of Hebron. They took all of their belongings with them, abandoning their homes, and established squatters' rights in Hebron.

The government was angry and embarrassed but hesitant to take a forceful action against fellow-Jews, for whom they felt a deep inner sympathy, however much they deplored their lawlessness. The squatters were persuaded, finally, to leave the Park Hotel, and to move into the army compound at Hebron while their case was being studied.

After deliberation, the Cabinet in Jerusalem decided to authorize the establishment of a new settlement at Kiryat Arba, in the Hebron district.

Kiryat Arba is now considered to be a development town, in the category of Dimona, although it is nothing like Dimona in any other respect. Dimona was created in the wilderness, with no history of conflict, no religious symbolism or artifacts to inflame passions. Nor is Dimona a city of militant Zionists, whereas in Hebron one finds zealots as militant as the ancient tribe of Zealots whose name entered all languages as the word for militancy.

* * *

The bus ride from Jerusalem to Hebron takes just under an hour. The route runs through Bethlehem and Gush Etzion (a group of two kibbutzim). The Jewish settlers of Hebron live in Kiryat Arba, one of the Biblical names of the area, about a mile and a half outside Arab Hebron. The bus stops in front of the *memshala,* the military government headquarters. It consists of a cluster of barracks and administrative buildings surrounded by barbed wire.

It is there that the Jewish settlers of Hebron lived for close to three years, until Rosh Hashana, 1971, when most of them were moved into the newly completed *shikunim,* the frontier housing units.

When we visited Kiryat Arba, there were two hundred and fifty completed units; thirty-five to forty families were living there, with the rest of the two hundred and fifty family units due for occupancy by the late fall of 1972. There was already a waiting list for new units scheduled to be built; there is never a lack of candidates for new-town housing in Israel. The people there talked about "the first five thousand settlers," as if five thousand were a starting-off point for further settlement, although the future status of Hebron, insofar as national sovereignty was concerned, was—theoretically, at least—not decided.

One has only to go to a settlement like Hebron—to see and feel the fervor of the people, witness their labors and sacrifice to clear the scrub desert and build a town and a life —to know that all talk in universities or political councils about the territories and future boundaries and the price of peace is just so much talk. The new settlements in Hebron, in the Gaza Strip, the kibbutzim in the Golan Heights—these are "facts," deliberately created to influence political decisions later on.

No matter what anyone told us politically, we became convinced that Hebron, the Golan, and parts, at least, of the Gaza Strip, would remain Israeli. They will not be given up, because no government would or could uproot the people who built these towns with the government's knowledge, consent, and help. We are not discussing the right or the wrong of this, but the fact of it.

Among the young couples, new Israelis, living at Kiryat Arba, are two—the Magenis and the Tors—whose lives, backgrounds, and personalities give a fair representation of the diverse peoples who come to Israel seeking a new life and who volunteer for frontier and new-development towns. We received a detailed report on these families and life in the settlement from one of the researchers who worked with us on this study: Judith Rubin, a friend and colleague of co-author Lucy Szekely, in the Research Department of ABC-TV News, in New York. Judith is herself a new immigrant in Israel and has provided us with much valuable information on the *olim,* as Israelis call the new immigrants.

\* \* \*

Chaim Mageni is twenty-six years old, married, father of two girls (aged two and one), originally from Brooklyn, New York City, educated at orthodox yeshivas, from grade school to the post-high school level. After high school in New York, he attended the Yeshiva Mercaz Harav Kook in Jerusalem.

He is a short, wiry man, about five feet five, very thin but sinewy, with dark blond hair, cut straight, of medium height. He has a short, patchy, blondish beard and dishwater gray-blue eyes. Chaim wears glasses and a *kipa*—a yarmulke or skullcap. He has a great deal of nervous energy, rocks back and forth when he talks, drums the table or chair with his fingers. He walks with long, bouncy strides, as though perpetually late for whatever he is doing.

Chaim first came to Israel in 1962, under the sponsorship of the B'nai Akiva movement (an orthodox Jewish group) to be educated as a trainer for leaders of the movement in the

United States. He completed his training, went back to begin his work in Boston, where he met and married his wife, Shoshana, then a student at Brandeis University. They were married in 1968, planning to earn some money in the States and then, as soon as possible, leave to immigrate to Israel. They are deeply religious, fervent Zionists, and Israeli nationalists.

They had been married three years when Judith interviewed them. Their elder daughter, Tiferet, was two, the younger daughter, Sima, was one, and, in the summer of '71, Shoshana was pregnant again. "God willing, a son." Shoshana's seventy-five-year-old grandmother from Boston (originally from England) was living with them in their settlement.

"At the time we came," Chaim recalled, "there were only six Jewish families in Hebron. We knew we were needed. Somebody has to do this job of resettling Jewish towns. We felt we had to volunteer to do it."

When asked what he meant by "somebody has to do this job," he replied, "The Divine Plan for the development of Israel calls for the return of Israel to the Jews."

When it was suggested that it was perhaps not that simple and that the frontiers of Israel had to be negotiated eventually, with decent respect for Arab rights, he stared coldly and said, "All the occupied territories need to be and will be eventually resettled by the Jews. There was a Jewish community living in Shechem [Nablus] until 1942, and there will be one again. I accept the Halachic ruling and I refuse to quote any boundaries for Eretz Israel. My conception of the State of Israel would certainly include Hebron and the entire West Bank."

There was little room for pursuing any discussion with Chaim about frontiers. It was apparent that the Bible was his atlas, and, beyond the Bible, any Jewish settlements in any area where Jews had settled were, ipso facto, Jewish. The simplicity of his self-righteous views was both enviable and irritating. "We are witness to the beginning of the redemption of the Jewish people," Chaim proclaimed, his eyes flashing and rolling, his finger pointing to heaven.

\* \* \*

One of the heroes of the Zionist nationalists is a former Air Force Chief, General Ezer Weizmann, whose planes won the Six-Day War in the first six hours, or, if that is an exaggeration, made the six-day victory possible in the first six hours by destroying the Egyptian Air Force, thus clearing the field for Israeli tanks and infantry. Since the battlefields of the Sinai are wide open, with no cover, it is essential to control the air and Weizmann's planes did that.

Weizmann told us, at a dinner party in Tel Aviv, that "Hebron is a Jewish city and will remain part of Israel. We will not let it go just because the U.N.—and what makes them God?—put Hebron on the Jordanian side of the line in the partition plan of 1947. The government in Jerusalem is weak, vacillating, and hypocritical when it appoints an Arab from Nazareth as a Deputy Minister of Health while not insisting that Hebron is an Israeli city. Is Nazareth more Israeli than Hebron?"

Weizmann's eyes shone and his strong voice boomed as he asserted: "The present situation is ideal and we should not be in a rush to negotiate, certainly not through Jarring, the U.N., or the U.S. State Department. Right now we have no official specific boundaries. All right, that's not terrible. We control our de-facto frontiers. There is no war, no fighting, no shelling, and we are strong.

"During this period, we are consolidating our territories, creating peace through facts, not on paper or in palavers. We are winning over the Arabs who live among us by giving them jobs, investment money, education, and health services. Our Arab neighbors see what's going on, you can be sure. One by one, they'll come to talk to us and then we will work out peace.

"And we don't need advice from Russians who send their armies into Hungary and Czechoslovakia, or America which sends its men and planes to Vietnam. They are not fighting for national survival but for power reasons. We are fighting for survival. It is life or death for us. Who are they to give us lessons?"

A new Israeli like Chaim Mageni speaks in terms identical to the older generation of the Weizmanns, adding to the General's nationalist militancy the special fervor of the orthodox Jew, seeing a Divine Plan in which he is a soldier of the redemption.

Chaim's wife, Shoshana, is as militant as Chaim, an assertive, arrogant Amazon of Israel.

During afternoon prayers, when the men were at the synagogue and the women preparing the evening meal, Shoshana took Judith Rubin aside and said, "Now it is time for us to talk. Tell me, what has been your Jewish education?"

"Well, I went to Hebrew school for a year, when I was six, and then to a Yiddish school for two years, when I was seven and eight. My father is deeply religious and I did not want to offend him, so I observed most of the ritual. But I felt I was not destined for a religious life and my father did not seek to impose his own ways upon me, so he let me follow my way. The same with my brother, who went to a Yeshiva grammar school, then to the regular New York school system."

"Aha," said Shoshana, her eyes gleaming with messianic fervor, "just as I thought, no proper Jewish education; you have no background."

Shoshana paid no attention to the flush of anger on Judith's cheeks.

"It is too bad that your parents were failures. You know, parents must teach a child three things, according to the Torah. They must teach a child a trade, how to swim, and the Torah itself. Your parents obviously did not teach you

Torah, so that I must call them failures."

Judith wondered what Shoshana would say if she knew that her parents had not even taught her how to swim, let alone a trade.

"I don't really see where it is any concern of yours to call my parents anything," Judith protested. "It seems to me that I, at least, learned how to be a human being and treat others as such, which to me is the essence of the Torah, anyway—and which, I regret, is more than many religious persons, thoroughly versed in the letter of the Torah, seem to have learned. After all, the Torah is the spirit of Jewish humanity, not just the letter of laws."

"No, no, no," said Shoshana, frowning and sighing heavily. "Let me tell you why I have a right to speak to you this way and to call your parents failures. More than a right, I have a duty to do so. The Torah says that if you see someone on the wrong path, or making a mistake, you must correct them and help them. I am simply doing a *mitzvah*—a blessing, a good deed—in showing you where you and your parents erred."

At this point, the men returned from *shul* and, to Judith's relief, Shoshana was distracted from further performance of her *mitzvah*.

\*     \*     \*

The Tor family was just as devout as the Magenis but less arrogantly messianic.

Ari Tor, in his mid-twenties, is an Israeli, born and bred. He is religious and nationalist and believes that Israel must keep all the occupied territories. "It is *asur*—forbidden—to return our lands.

"We want peace, of course, but the question is what is peace? A real peace has less to do with territories than with a desire to live in peace. Where is that desire? Did it manifest itself when Hebron was in the hands of Jordan? Were they peaceful then? Why should we believe they would be peaceful now if we gave them back land on which they did not live in peace before? Did they accept peace when the U.N. proposed peace? Why should we believe that now they will obey the U.N. when they never did before? No, no, if they want peace, then they will come to us to make peace and we will make peace with them. Handing over lands will not do it."

Yona Tor agreed with her husband. She is not Israeli-born but, perhaps for that reason, is even more fervently, patriotically Israeli.

Yona is twenty-three and came to Israel alone from Argentina at the age of thirteen, in the Youth Aliya movement. Later her parents immigrated and are now living in B'nai Brak. The conversations with Yona were conducted in Spanish.

Yona has a newborn child and wants "several more." She is a teacher at Kiryat Arba.

"I came to Israel for nationalistic reasons."

"Do you mean religious reasons—that is, because you wanted to live a full Jewish life?"

"Religious? Nationalistic? Is there a difference? When I say nationalistic I mean religious, but if I say religious I also mean nationalistic. I do not see the distinction. We Jews are a nation and Judaism is our religion.

"In Argentina, my family always talked about Palestine, and then, after 1948, about Israel, as 'our country,' 'the homeland.' Israel was always part of my life, even when I was living in Argentina. I am not an Argentinian. I am a Jew who happened, for a while, to be living in Argentina."

Yona, a diligent housewife, whose small flat is always shining, without a speck of the dust that covers everything in Hebron, kept looking around the room while talking, as though to challenge anything to be out of place.

"We came to Hebron because it is important that this ancient Jewish city be settled again by Jews. We did not lose eternal rights because once we were driven out."

(Curiously, none of those who kept repeating this logical argument seemed aware of the fact that this is exactly what the Palestinian Arabs say about having been driven out of of their lands. When we pointed this out, the usual answer was "Oh, if they accept Israel, they can come back. We will work it out one day.")

"Many of the new settlers here are not orthodox and that does create some problems. The majority of the country is not very religious. But they are all Jews, and they all give their children a Jewish education and everyone learns Bible history in school. It is not enough for the Magenis, and I, too, would like to see more. But we must accept what is. And there is strength in diversity. The mix is good here. Mix! It's funny to say mix—after all, we are all Jews. And we are devoted to Israel. It will work out."

*        *        *

Once again, an interview had ended with the words "It will work out." Just as, so often, after listening to discussions of problems and controversies, we would hear, "But we will solve it, we will solve it."

The basic strength and stability of Israeli society seemed to us to be beyond doubt, capable of resisting the many strains of security and social conflicts.

There is also no doubt that religious differences are a major issue of controversy among Israelis.

The Continuing Survey, of the Institute of Applied Social Research, conducted two national samplings on religious questions in 1971, and has provided us with the breakdown of replies for those over and under thirty.

CONTINUING SURVEY:
QUESTION B3—Relations between religious and nonreligious citizens

There exist divergent opinions
among Jews on the problem of

religion in Israel. Do you think
that at present relations between
religious and nonreligious
Jews are good?

|  | Youth<br>% | Adults<br>% |
| --- | --- | --- |
| Very good | 1 | 3 |
| Good enough | 10 | 17 |
| Not so good | 54 | 51 |
| Not good at all | 35 | 29 |
|  | 100 | 100 |

CONTINUING SURVEY:
QUESTION B4—The practice of religion

Do you customarily observe
Jewish tradition?

|  | Youth<br>% | Adults<br>% |
| --- | --- | --- |
| Yes, absolutely; I try to observe it<br>in detail | 10 | 15 |
| I try to observe most religious<br>tradition | 8 | 12 |
| I observe Jewish tradition in part | 46 | 47 |
| I do not observe Jewish tradition<br>at all | 36 | 26 |
|  | 100 | 100 |

The figures leave no doubts: nine out of ten young Israelis believe that religious relations are not very good and eight out of ten said they were not devout in the practice of religion or even tradition.

The largest groups, both youth and adults, observe the rituals only partly or not at all. It is particulary interesting to note that those who observe tradition totally are greater in number than those who observe largely. One is either or-thodox and observes the law in full or inclines to break away.

Almost every specialist on the question told us that the an-swers to the words "in part" used in the questionnaire tended very much to mean minimal: the lighting of candles; more or less observance of dietary laws, rather than strict observance; the celebration of the most important holidays and memorial services for families and closer friends; the symbols of reli-gion rather than religion itself.

The high correlation of Israelis who are not devout—eight out of ten—leaves one wondering just why the laws on kosher food, on the Sabbath, and other religious statutes are so strict and widely observed.

A government information officer told us that the answer is political, not religious.

"The ruling coalition has a narrow majority in the Knesset. The few votes of religious parliamentarians can spell the dif-ference between passage or rejection of a bill, indeed of the maintenance in power of the government itself. With so nar-row a majority of the ruling coalition, even a very small minority can wield very great power.

"It was once said of the United States that it was a Protes-tant country dominated by a Catholic minority. Well, we are all Jews, of course. But one can say that Israel is a cultural society dominated by a religious minority."

# X I

## The New Israelis
## and Zionism

Thus saith the Lord of hosts; Behold, I will
save my people from the east country, and
from the west country; and I will bring them,
and they shall dwell in the midst of Jerusalem. . . .

—ZECHARIAH 8:7–8.

Aliya!

The literal Hebrew meaning of the word *"aliya"* is "the ascent." It is the word used to mean "immigration" and its adaption in this usage illustrates the passion, the fervor of Jews contemplating a new life in the Jewish homeland. It is, for them, an ascent to a heaven on earth. That life is hard in Israel—not paradisaical, in fact—in no way alters the emotional validity of the notion that immigration, *aliya,* is an ascent from almost two thousand years of life in the depths of persecution, intolerance, and exile, ending the sufferings of the pariah.

In this twentieth century, the waves of *aliya* that carried Jews from every corner of the world back to the ancient homeland is a chapter of history as stirring as any in the Bible. At the dawn of this century, in 1900, there were 50,000 Jews living in Turkish Palestine. They were an infinitesimal minority compared to the Jews living in the world outside, in the non-Jewish world, which the Jews call the Diaspora, or the Gola: 50,000 out of a total world Jewish population of 10,700,000, a mere 0.5% living in Palestine.

By the census of 1969, the proportion of Jews living in Israel, in their own homeland, rose to 18%: 2,497,000 Jews in Israel out of 13,876,000 Jews in the world. The increase from 50,000 in 1900 to about 2,500,000 in 1969 is an increase of fiftyfold, while the percent of proportion between Jews in Israel and the world increased thirty-sixfold.

When the State of Israel was founded in 1948, the total Jewish population of the country was only about 650,000. From 1948 to 1970, these 650,000 Jews had to absorb into their society 750,000 new citizens born in Israel and 1,100,-000 immigrants who "ascended" to Israel. In other words, something more than a half-million people had to welcome, support, educate, care for, and defend almost two million newcomers in the space of only two decades. There is no equivalent in all human history of this magnificent performance by the Jews of Israel and their fellow-Jews around the world, without whose total support the miracle of *aliya* would not have come to pass.

A multiplicity of Jewish organizations around the world all contributed, but the greatest contribution came, of course, from the strongest and richest of the world's Jewish communities, the American Jews.

There was some help from governments—the Germans, in the form of restitution payments for Jewish properties, and credits and loans, in addition to credits and grants from the American government—but Israel's heavy defense expenditures offset government aid. (It should be noted that the American government also gave credits, loans, and military grants to Arab governments, balancing aid to Israel, an aid cruelly overbalanced in favor of the Arabs by the massive, multibillion-dollar Soviet military and economic aid program to the Arab nations.)

The bulwark of Israel was thrown up by private citizens, not by governments. The greatest charitable and investment-loan campaign ever carried out has been achieved in the last year and a half, when leaders of the world Jewish community have been redeeming their pledge to raise a billion dollars, in United Jewish Appeal grants, State of Israel bond sales, and a plethora of philanthropic devices designed to succor Jews throughout the world as well as in Israel.

The decision to set the billion-dollar goal, which officials in charge themselves feared was an impossible dream, was inspired by the magic word *"aliya,"* and most particularly by the first signs that the doors of Russia, behind which 3,000,000 Jews are being subjected to intense pressures to assimilate, were at long last beginning to swing open.

In the years 1960–1969, less than 10,000 Jews had been

able to leave the Soviet Union, most of them very old or very young. But in 1970 came the promise that conditions would be eased up and that an average of 100 Jews a day, and even more, could go to Israel.

Hymns of thanksgiving were sung in the synagogues of Israel, in the synagogues of the world, for all Jews have mourned for their brothers and sisters in the Soviet Union.

In New York, Rabbi Meir Kahane, a storm center of controversy in the Jewish world with his militant Jewish Defense League, seized upon a slogan that would make even his most bitter critics cheer: "Never Again!" The world's Jews vowed that never again would they be silent; never again would they submit to the terror that sent six million Jews to the ovens in Germany. Not that they were accusing the Russians of sending Jews to the ovens, but they did accuse the Russians of a crime which they regarded as second only to Hitler's physical genocide: the crime of spiritual genocide, of attempting to wipe out the Jewish religion in Russia.

It takes enormous courage for a Soviet Jew even to indicate his desire to leave Russia, and this statement of intent is but the first step in a long, frustrating, fearful chain of events. Once a Jew in Russia reveals his interest in going to Israel, he puts in jeopardy his job, the education of his children, or his own education if he is a student. He is frequently picked up by the security police and brought in for "questioning" or submitted to "psychological and mental testing" to establish his sanity.

Every newspaper reader, radio or television listener has heard dozens of stories of distinguished educators, scientists, even a member of the Soviet Academy of Science, who have been dismissed from their posts and subjected to daily harassment, as well as accounts of the shocking "ransom" demands, revealed by reporters in the summer of 1972, of payments for exit permits, ranging from $1,000 to $25,000, according to the higher-education degrees the applicant holds.

There is little if any opportunity for a Soviet Jew to express his religious spirit, although his papers and identifications are all stamped with the word "Jew." There are no Yeshivas (Jewish religious schools), no seminaries in the Soviet Union. For Russia's three million Jews there are only sixty-five authorized synagogues. Jews are forbidden to publish periodicals and devotional materials, not even prayer books or Bibles.

There are some who say, "Well, that's terrible, but it is Russia's internal affair. If they want to stamp out religion, according to their communist dogma, that's their business." To which the Jews of the world reply: "If Russia wants to suppress Judaism, it does not give the Soviets the right to suppress Jews. If they don't want Jews, then let our people go!"

For world Jewry, for the government in Israel, the question of immigration into Israel is a human right, the right of all peoples, of any faith, to live and worship where and how they wish. It is this basic human right, subscribed to in the United Nations Charter by all nations, including Russia, which the Soviet authorities have been violating.

The passion of the Soviet Jew was expressed by Professor Michael Zand when he finally emigrated to Israel: "I had everything in the Soviet Union, but I was a privileged slave among slaves. I was deprived of my human freedom and my Jewish identity. Don't say, 'Let my people live.' They can't live as Jews in the Soviet Union. Say, 'Let my people go!'"

Slowly, they came out, 1,000 a year, then the quickening pace at the turn of 1970: 20,000, then 30,000.

No one outside the Kremlin walls knows why the Russians suddenly began to open the doors—not yet wide open, to be sure, or without enormous difficulties and dangers, but the first real opening with the hope of more. Was it rising pressure and unrest by brave Soviet Jews? The courage of those who declared themselves must have been a big factor. Was it Rabbi Kahane and his harassment of Soviet diplomats in New York? His partisans say yes, his detractors say no.

Whatever the truth, one cannot deny that the doors began to swing open right after Kahane's militants pounded on them.

Officials in Jerusalem talk cautiously; they do not want to risk impeding the flow. As one said to us, "Never mind why. What is important is that everything be done to help bring them out and help them to a new life in Israel."

And that is the rub.

It is one thing to throb heartfully about the ascent to the paradise of a Jewish homeland; it is something very different to cope with the earthly reality of absorbing new immigrants in great numbers, while coping with all the other social, economic, and military problems of the young State of Israel.

First, there is the financial cost of paying the exit visas, transporting the new immigrant, who comes out of Russia with only $100, a suitcase, his skills and hopes, first to the transit center at Schönau, in Austria, then to Lod Airport, outside Tel Aviv. The minimum exit visa for an emigrant without advanced degrees is $1,000. Then each immigrant family must be taken to an absorption and educational center. Most Russian Jews today do not speak Hebrew or even Yiddish. They must learn a new language, be given a home, find a job.

A thoroughly unexpected development, in the early days of immigration, was the discovery that even highly educated men or skilled craftsmen had to be taught a completely new way of thinking. Officials tell the poignant story of a skilled Russian leather artisan. He is the kind of man who can earn his way very quickly, for there is a shortage of true craftsmen in his specialties.

The Jewish Agency promptly gave the shoemaker a loan so that he might set up his own business, buy equipment, furnish his shop. He was overjoyed and rushed out to make his purchases. A week later, he came back to the agency, thanked them for what they had done for him, told them his shop was ready, and then asked, "When will you send me the customers?"

It had never occurred to him that finding customers would be his responsibility.

Some Russian immigrants are more sophisticated than the shoe craftsman, some less. All of them, however, are displaced and require great expenditures and social training to adjust to life in Israel.

The cost of equipping a new immigrant to live his own life in Israel averages out to about $20,000 for a family of four, although some statisticians say the true cost is much higher, nearer to $10,000 a head, depending upon how certain state services are calculated. Let us agree on an average figure of $7,500 a head. If, as hoped, 50,000 new immigrants come this year, then the total cost, over and above all budget items, is $375,000,000, all of it to be raised from private citizens.

Israeli and American Zionist officials insist that most of the Jewish money to Israel goes for the saving of human beings, not for guns, not for war, as Arab propagandists and anti-Israel critics falsely charge. Israel, they say, defends herself, raises her own money for guns, and her own sons to man the guns. The Israelis do not ask Americans to fight for them, as the South Vietnamese do. They get no help from Russia, as the Arabs do. They take care of themselves. But they cannot do that and also take care of all the victims of oppression who seek a new life in Israel. The return to Israel, the ultimate aim of Zionism—this is the responsibility of the entire world Jewish community and of those non-Jews—and there are some—who are sensitive to the long sufferings of the Jews and wish to make their contribution, too.

They reject the argument put forward to the effect that the Jewish philanthropic and investment programs for Israel permit the Israelis to spend all their money on guns and defense. This specious argument, they say, overlooks the fact that Israel has no choice but to defend herself or die. Thus, if there were no Jewish philanthropy, there would be no *aliya*, no immigration.

The Israelis would not stop defending themselves; they would, with broken hearts, have to close the gates. So Jewish philanthropy does not permit military efforts; it is designed for and used exclusively for humanitarian purposes, and even the money does not relieve the very great strain that immigration absorption imposes upon Israeli society, a strain that becomes immediately apparent when one questions young Israelis about *aliya* and Zionism.

"Yes, let them come, all Jews, from anywhere, whatever they may be, religious or not religious, scholars and fishmongers, let them all come, for Israel is the one sure refuge of the Jew."

The speaker, Avraham Golan, himself came to Israel in the great wave of the *aliya* in 1952, from Rumania. His parents were lower-middle-class clerks. He is a medical student in his fifth year of studies.

"Never could a Jew in my circumstances have become a medical student in Rumania, unless—and there are few such exceptions—I had been a fervent communist. In Israel, my fervor is for medicine and for freedom. I am not religious but I feel very much a Jew, at home with fellow-Jews in a true homeland. Other Jews in the world should have the same chance I had, so I am in favor of continued *aliya* to Israel.

"No, I am not a Zionist. Listen, you must get this right, for there is much confusion about it. A Zionist believes there is no true Jewish life outside Zion; that a Jew in the Diaspora is not completely a Jew. A true Zionist thinks every Jew should come to Israel.* I do not think so. I think every Jew who *wants* to come to Israel should come and be helped to come. But if he does not want to come, then let him stay where he is and let him be our brother in the world."

* This statement is not correct. It is not a principle of Zionism that all Jews must or should settle in Israel. Some militant Zionists do argue this but it is highly controversial and certainly not an official principle of the World Zionist Congress.

Avraham told us that he supported the government program of encouraging Jews to come to Israel, even though the cost of immigration is a very heavy burden for each working, taxpaying citizen of Israel. "We *are* our brother's keeper, at whatever cost. That is the lesson of the holocaust. 'Never Again!'—that is the slogan; it must never happen again."

\*　　\*　　\*

Aliza Gorkani, age twenty-eight, born in Israel of parents who had emigrated from Morocco, had strong reservations about immigration. She is a high school graduate, with one year of university, lives in a typical Moroccan-Jewish family of eight in small quarters in Tel Aviv, and is resentful of the government's preoccupation with new immigrants, particularly from Russia, at the expense, she believes, of older immigrants.

"The *olim,* the new immigrants, are getting too much, and we, the Sephardim, who came twenty years ago—we are the forgotten people of Israel. We live in slums, we live in the same small flats they gave us twenty years ago; they do nothing for us. But the Russians come in, they demand everything, they get new housing, spacious quarters. It is not just.

"Only true Zionists should be allowed to come. I mean those who are really Jewish, who yearn to live Jewish lives, rather than just those who are seeking to exchange one kind of life for another.

"The Russians come here and they grumble and complain and demand. Instead of going to a kibbutz or a new town, they want to stay in Tel Aviv or Jerusalem—already overcrowded. They say, 'If we don't get what we want, we'll go back to Russia.' And some of them have gone back to Russia. Well, I say if they don't like it here, let them go back where they came from. And when they want to stay here, then let them start at the bottom the way my parents did when they came from Morocco. We should get the new apartments and the Russians should take ours.

"The young Russian boys and girls are fine; they are ready for a new life. But it is the older ones, the doctors and professors and technicians—they think they are better than anyone, they are snobs, they look down on us. We don't want them.

"We like the American *olim* better, even though they also grumble a lot about social problems. The Americans, particularly the young, have a chip on their shoulder. But many of them have given up very good social positions and money in America and come here with true idealism, so I admire them.

"The Russians do not come as idealists. They are not coming *for* Israel, but to get *away from* Russia. That's a good reason for them, but not for us. They should come to us out of love for Israel and a willingness to sacrifice for that love. Then they would be good *olim*."

*        *        *

We were surprised by Aliza's vehemence and bitterness. We had heard complaints about Russian immigrants before, generally from those, like Aliza, of Sephardic origin, especially Moroccan—they are the most dissatisfied and complaining of Israeli citizens—but nothing like her sharp resentments. Perhaps that is simply a matter of personality or temperament in her case.

We did discover, as our investigations proceeded, and Russian immigration increased, that the jealousies and rivalries between old and new settlers, even between young native Israelis and the immigrants, were wider and deeper than is generally admitted. This conflict of interests is contained, however, by the majority sentiment of hatred for Soviet tyranny and the even broader and deeper sympathy for and identification with the Soviet Jew, particularly among the Ashkenazim, whose own parents originally came from Russia and Eastern Europe. There is another aspect of support for Soviet immigration at very high levels which transcends the Sephardic complaint. It was voiced to me by Minister of Transportation and Communications, Shimon Peres, one of the leaders of Israel.

"We are doing everything we can, and will do more, to eliminate social injustices and inequities. We admit that there are difficulties. How could there not be, with the terrible costs of defense and all our other services?"

Peres set his strong jaw, and he clenched his fists as he added, "But we have a duty to every Jew who seeks freedom in Israel and we will do our duty without being dissuaded by grumblers. And let this be clear, very clear: the new immigrants are not only coming to be rescued by us, they are bringing to us the highest skills in the world. We need them as much as they need us, and we are going to do everything that needs to be done to make them happy and successful in their work, for themselves and for Israel."

Peres relaxed, smiled shyly, a bit embarrassed by his outburst.

"Do not think me hard. You know I am not. But a government must sometimes be very firm while being compassionate. We know about the complaints of those who say they have lived in inadequate housing. We know that old housing is not as good as our new housing. But to charge that we discriminate against Afro-Asian Jews in favor of European Jews is not true. It hurts to hear such charges. If a Moroccan comes today, does he not get the same housing as a Russian?

"Of course, there is less immigration now from Arab lands and more from Russia. That is simply an historical development. It is not discrimination. We cannot stop or reverse the flow. Nor can we ask immigrants from Russia, or America, who come from urban centers and a high standard of education, culture, and living to lower their standards. Why should they?

"The scientists and high-level technicians get many excellent offers of housing and employment—in Australia and other countries. Many can have a brilliant career and life in America. We want them in Israel and they want to be in Israel, so we must all do the best we can.

"As for those who claim inequities, they should be and are being helped—and they could, perhaps, do more to help themselves. But, believe me, nothing will stop our encouragement to the *aliya* of Jews."

\*     \*     \*

Simon, age twenty-five, handsomely dark, lithe, a "Latin-lover" type, was born in Israel of Spanish parents. He himself looks like a young bullfighter, moving gracefully but with a swagger. He showed his white teeth in a broad smile as he leaned across the bar he tends in Tel Aviv and chatted with us.

"You know, we Mediterranean types like to complain. And, in truth, there is much to complain about. But, as a Jew in Israel, I'm a lot better off than my parents were in Toledo.

"Look, I'll tell you the truth, I've no appetite for fighting —maybe I'm even a coward—so I told the army that I am a conscientious objector. I am, I hate war and fighting. So they told me, 'Okay, you don't want to go into the army, so don't come.' How do you like that? Now, you can't complain about a country like this.

"Let the immigrants come, I'll pay my taxes; that's the least I can do for my country."

\*     \*     \*

Sami, Shmuel, and Yoav are Yemenites, who, of all the Afro-Asian Jews, have best assimilated and integrated into Israeli life.

They serve as policemen, soldiers, laborers, dockers, truckers. Some of the earliest immigrants almost literally came out of caves in Yemen. Even immigrant flats were palaces to them. Some had to be taught how to use a fork. In one generation, their sons have moved high and fast up the social scale of their family history, however low their relative scale may be in Israeli society.

Sami, age twenty-two, was born in Israel. His family came from Aden in 1935. His parents are deeply religious Jews, very conservative citizens. Not Sami. Sami is, in his modest way, a "swinger." He works as a truck driver, has his own apartment, a record player, with a big collection of records, enough pocket money to go to cafés a few nights a week and a restaurant on the weekend.

Like many new Israelis, Sami is a chain-smoker—three packs a day—claims he does not smoke "hash," although most of his friends do. His apartment is a one-room-kitchenette-bath in the Hatikva section of Tel Aviv, a tenement area, not much above slum level, but for Sami it is a real home. He tries to beautify his little flat with posters and his record player is always on, with his favorite American "soul" music.

Sami has ten brothers and sisters. They were born and raised in a kibbutz, where he lived for six years. As they achieve their majority, they all try to make their way to the big city. Sami loves Tel Aviv and Israel. He is, like most Yemenites we met, fervently nationalistic, proud of Israel, deeply mistrustful of the Arabs. "No Jew should live in an Arab land. They should all come to Israel and we should help them in every way," Sami told us.

Shmuel is twenty-one, also born in Israel. He is just out of the army, where, he told us proudly, "I was a paratrooper." He is, like Sami and most other Yemenites we saw, lean, muscular, dark-skinned, with black eyes, graceful and handsome. He operates a tractor on a *moshav* and earns the almost incredible salary for Israel of $10,000 a year. He works a fourteen- to sixteen-hour day, revels in it, but told us, "I am saving my money so that I can open up a shop in Tel Aviv."

Like Sami, he, too, is nationalistic, and all through our

evening together—Lucy and Robert Szekely invited them to their apartment for a Hungarian goulash dinner—kept insisting that we must emigrate to Israel. "How can you live anywhere else; this is the greatest country in the world. You're Jewish, aren't you? Why aren't you here with us?"

Yoav was one of the few Yemenites who could not be cast in a movie. Aged twenty, he was more shy than the others, slighter of build, ill at ease. He is still in the army and intends to enlist as a professional soldier when his conscription duty ends.

He was born in Israel, has four brothers and sisters. His father works in a paper factory. He told us that they spoke only Arabic at home, for his parents had never become fluent in Hebrew, although he himself finished high school and intends to go on to become an electrical engineer in the army.

"Where else could I get such opportunities as the army is offering me? This is the country of the Jews and for the Jews. We must support the government's immigration policy," Yoav asserted.

Strangely, he boasted, with evident pride, "I have an uncle in the United States. He is very successful there." It seemed not to occur to him that there was a conflict between his Zionism and his pride in his American uncle, who, he seemed to feel, gave him a certain social status.

\*　　\*　　\*

Ilana, age twenty-two, born in Israel of German parents, works in the public-relations department of Tel Aviv University. Her father is a high-ranking bureaucrat in civil aviation. She hopes to start law studies next year. Ilana volunteered for army service, although she was entitled to exemption for medical reasons.

"The army was a marvelous experience. I'm glad they took me, gave me my chance to serve my country. I had a responsible job as drill instructor. It helped me mature, to find myself; it gave me confidence. The university can wait.

I'll be a better student next year, after the army and a year's work here in the office."

Ilana is a self-assured young woman and holds strong opinions on almost every subject we broached, particularly on Zionism and immigration problems:

"My father worked hard and by himself to come to Israel. He paid for his own ticket, and rented, then bought an apartment, working hard all the time. I know they like to say, 'Oh, that's very German,' but why should a German Jew work harder than a Moroccan Jew? We are all Jews, aren't we? The trouble with new immigrants now is that they want everything done for them, given to them, while they don't have to do anything. It isn't fair.

"Oh, the Sephardim are always saying that we aren't fair to them, that they don't get good apartments. Well, my father did not *get* a good apartment. He earned it; he merited it by his own work. My parents worked hard all their lives. They are suffering in health because of the hard years. But still they work, and they are still paying off the mortgage on our place.

"Why can't the Sephardim do that? Why can't they work and pay a mortgage? All they do is make children and ask the state to support them. That is not a good immigration. They shouldn't complain about the Russian Jews who are coming. They will make wonderful citizens of Israel, will make their way, most of them. That's the kind of *olim* the country can afford."

\* \* \*

Hanach, an attractive young married woman of twenty-four, also works at Tel Aviv University. She took her bachelor's degree in sociology, is married to a young instructor, who finished law and is taking his master's in political science while teaching undergraduate courses. They were both born in Israel of immigrant parents.

Hanach is an ardent Zionist.

"All Jews should come to Israel. They might be able to live well in the Diaspora, in France or America, but not a complete Jewish life. I have no patience with those who complain about the 'burden.' Is my fellow-Jew a 'burden' or a human being? How can a Jew with a knowledge of our people's history of persecution complain about the cost of immigration?

"There is plenty of space in Israel for all the Jews of the world. If it takes time to build flats or houses, well, while waiting, let us take our fellow-Jews into our own homes. I would take five Jews into my little apartment. Let everyone do his share.

"There is no great problem of assimilation. Look how few our parents were when the state was founded in 1948. They took in more than a million, plus the birth of their own children. We absorbed and assimilated hundreds of thousands from Africa and Asia in the fifties. Sure, it was a bit difficult. Where does it say it should be easy? But no one can tell me it cannot be done. It can be done. It should be done.

"I hope they open wide the gates of Russia. There are some who say we will drown in the flood of Russian Jews. I say to them, 'Open up the floodgates and you will see how Jews can float on the tides of freedom!' "

\*     \*     \*

We found that more than 90% of those to whom we spoke supported fully or in good measure the general principle that all Jews who want to come to Israel should be able to come, and helped to come if personally unable to make it. Where we struck controversy was over Zionist principles: that all Jews *should* come to Israel, and that the government should have an active program of encouragement to *aliya*.

More than half of those we interviewed said they were not Zionists and disagreed with the pursuit of an active program.

The prevailing majority sentiment was expressed by an Israeli of twenty-seven, Pinhas Mousateff, whose father came from Russia, mother from Panama, and wife from France: "Some will come from conviction, others by eviction, and we should welcome them all, but none should come by seduction, for they will expect too much and get too little. Israel is the homeland for Jews who seek it, not a recruiting organization for immigrants."

The controversy over immigration is clearly inseparable from the social strains between the Sephardim and the Ashkenazim. Without that rivalry and jealousy, the program of *aliya* would be more popular, cause less resentment. But, as with most of the great public issues of Israel, the controversy does not seriously threaten the unity of the country or the fabric of its society, and has little effect or none on the government's activist program of *aliya*.

The desire to force open the gates of the Soviet Union, coupled with a strong push to persuade high-level American talents to come to Israel—these are major objectives, well beyond the level of the current public debate.

Hanach's passionate cry, "Open up the floodgates and you will see how Jews can float on the tides of freedom," is an emotion shared by most Jews, whatever reservations they may have about the modalities of immigration.

There is one psychological aspect to the question of *aliya* that one finds often enough among Jews in Western countries, particularly France and the United States: the deep-rooted fear that Zionism will eventually result in a recrudescence of anti-Semitism. We sensed this most often in French Jews, particularly those at the higher levels of French society. They rarely put their fear into precise words, but it was apparent in the background of their objections.

What they fear most is the possibility that, under pressure of Zionists, the anti-Semites will simply say, "Why don't all you Jews go to Israel, and then we can all live in peace?"

One French friend, more candid than most, with a very Gallic sense of irony, put it this way: "Someone is sure to tell me to go back to where I didn't come from."

This fear arises out of a long history of Jews being told to go back somewhere else and out of a misconception about the relationship between Jews in Israel and Jews in the Diaspora, a misconception compounded by misunderstandings about Zionism.

The original motivation of the Zionists was to create a Jewish homeland, to succor all Jews suffering from persecution, but not necessarily to *require* all Jews to move to Zion. However, the rhetoric of militant Zionists soon led to the belief that all Jews should go to Israel, must go to Israel.

There is a wide margin of difference between "be able to," "should," and "must." The majority of Israelis would subscribe to the principle "be able to go to Israel"; they are divided about whether Jews "should" go; only a small minority believes that all Jews "must" go to Israel to live a truly Jewish life.

At a luncheon in Paris with pre-eminent intellectual leaders of the Jewish community, we heard a famous editor say to a famous writer, a member of the French Academy, "But I am a Frenchman first, a Jew afterward."

"Sure you are, in your mind," said the writer, "but not in the mind of your fellow-Frenchmen. Under Pétain we were all Jews first, Frenchmen much afterward."

The debate moved around the table for a long time, but no one made the point that should have been made: the issue is irrelevant, for a man must be what he thinks he is in many different domains and act according to his concepts, without trying to balance what cannot truly be balanced.

Is an Irishman a Catholic first, or an Irishman? It is, to push the argument to the ridiculous, almost—although not quite—like asking are you a fisheater or an American? The question of nationality versus Catholicism has finally been settled as a decisive political issue in America since the election of John F. Kennedy. It is surely time to settle it for the Jews.

A Jew can be a Jew and an American, or a Frenchman, or any other nationality where there is freedom and a man is accepted without reference to his faith. Each must decide for himself whether such freedom exists in his country. He must then decide what his true loyalties are. Only one thing has changed for Jews, changed fundamentally in the past two decades: Jews now have a place to go to if they are not wanted where they are.

And there is no doubt where Israel stands, no matter how much grumbling is heard behind the city walls: the gates of Israel are and will remain open.

# XII

## The New Israelis
## and Israel

*But thou, Israel, art my servant, Jacob whom I have chosen, the seed of Abraham my friend. . . . Behold, all they that were incensed against thee shall be ashamed and confounded. . . .*

—ISAIAH 41:8, 11.

M o s t of the young people who have been talking with us through these pages were not born, or were toddlers, when an event took place, on the twenty-ninth of November, 1947, that was to mark their lives and the lives of many citizens of the world: the decision taken at Flushing Meadows, by the young Organization of the United Nations, to partition the ancient land of Palestine into two new states, the State of Israel and the State of Palestine.

To judge from the nature of today's world debate on the Middle East and the propaganda of the anti-Israeli forces, almost everybody has forgotten the decision and the events that flowed from it. That decision was implemented only by half, with consequences that still threaten the peace of the area and of the world: the State of Israel was founded, the State of Palestine was not.

The failure to create the State of Palestine has left about a million Palestinians stateless, many of them homeless, burning with frustration and hatred, turning some of them into desperate, bloodthirsty terrorists, who, twenty-five years later, in the summer of 1972, massacred dozens of innocent people at Lod Airport and drowned the Olympic Games in blood.

But it was not the Jews of Israel who left them stateless. The leaders of Israel accepted, albeit with a heavy heart, the partition frontiers traced by the United Nations in 1947.

It was the leaders of Egypt, Transjordan, Syria, Iraq, and Lebanon who rejected the partition of Palestine. Their armies attacked the Jews soon after the U.N. decision, and the first Arab-Israeli war was fought savagely through the spring of 1948, until the truce of June.

The State of Israel was proclaimed, recognized by most of the countries in the world and accepted as a member of the United Nations.

But the State of Palestine was not proclaimed. Instead, the Arab armies remained on the armistice lines, occupying territory awarded to the Palestinians.

Transjordan—the name itself means "across the Jordan" —had sent its legions across the Jordan River, but did not recall them. The kingdom changed its name to Jordan and simply annexed the land, now called the West Bank and now occupied by the Israelis, as a result of the Six-Day War of 1967. Jordan demands the return of those occupied lands, not for the Palestinians but for itself.

Egypt, in 1948, occupied the Gaza Strip and never gave it back to the Palestinians. It lost the land to Israel in the Six-Day War and now demands it back, not for the Palestinians but for Egypt.

The homeless, stateless Palestinians, lusting for the blood of Israelis, were herded into camps and left to rot, not by the Jews but by their own Arab "brothers." The oil-rich Arabs could have given them homes and a new life, the way the much poorer Israelis gave homes and a new life to immigrant Jews. But they did not.

This is not to say that Israel is right in all of its policy positions or that Israel has the right to keep all of the territories won by conquest. As we have seen, many Israelis recognize the existence of injustices and of the need to make compromises and sacrifices for peace. It is to say, however, that Israel's right to exist, to live behind recognized and secure frontiers, free of harassment by neighbors, is both a legal and a moral human right, too often forgotten in the course of debate.

In these past twenty-five years, as the new generation of Israelis was born and bred in the new state, Israel has grown steadily stronger, despite all the wars and terrorism, and despite the shifting of alliances by the Russians and the French, once the stoutest supporters of Israel, now severe critics— some would say enemies. The Israelis understand the French interest in Arabian oil but are disappointed to note that the humanitarian French cannot rise above venal interests.

When the United Nations drafted the partition lines, it awarded some 8,000 square miles to the State of Israel, then a community of some 600,000 people. Today, Israel's population, by birth and immigration, has skyrocketed to more than 3,000,000, and the territory under its control has expanded to 34,000 square miles. Its final size and shape will be determined one day by peace negotiations with the Arabs, or simply by time itself, if the long period of no peace-no war continues, as seems likely for as far ahead as one can now see.

The nature of Israeli society has undergone and will undergo changes even more dramatic than those of its size and shape.

At birth, twenty-five years ago, Israel was an underdeveloped, rural country. Today, it is a fast-developing, industrial, urban society; less than 10% of its people are engaged in agriculture.

At birth, Israel's population was overwhelmingly of European origin. Today, more than half the people are of Afro-Asian origin.

At birth, Israel was a country of immigrants. Today, half of the population was born in Israel.

At birth, Israel was a cosmopolitan country, speaking all the major languages of the world. Today, Hebrew is the dominant language. Israelis look inward, not outward, are growing more provincial, less cosmopolitan, particularly those under thirty, the leaders of tomorrow.

At birth, Israel was motivated by utopian Zionist socialism. Today, Israel is a semi-capitalist—on its way to becoming a dominant capitalist—society. Its gates are still open for Jews, but Zionism is contested by many of the young and is a source of social friction. No longer utopian or ideological or even idealistic, Israel, as its young people told us, is becoming pragmatic, practical, and traditionalist rather than zealous in its politics and its religious practices.

No one person can speak for a country as varied as Israel and there is no single Israeli type who could encompass differences as great as those between Dafna Atlas, biophysicist, basketball player, upper-middle-class member of a prosperous scientific family, and Sami, the Yemenite truck driver. That is why we have presented so broad a spectrum of interviews and checked them against the national surveys.

But there was one interview with a remarkable young Israeli fairly representative of the majority opinion and of special interest because of his leadership role, particularly in public information. We referred briefly to this young Israeli earlier in the book. He is Gideon Samet, editor of *Ha'aretz*.

His words, thoughts, articulation, the way he works—all seemed to us a representation of the dominant type, rather than the stereotype, of the new Israeli. If people like Ben-Gurion and Golda Meir typify the original founders, if Moshe Dayan represents the first sabras, then Gideon Samet represents the leadership element among the first Israelis in almost two millenniums to be born and bred in the State of Israel, the new Israelis.

We felt that his words would be a logical conclusion to these interviews, for they give us a prefiguration of the future of Israel under the leadership of his generation.

\*     \*     \*

"There are three generations living side by side—or more precisely, layer upon layer, here in Israel. To understand Israel, one must understand the essential of each of the generations and how one evolved out of the other. They are distinguished by three different questions that motivated each in turn:

"*Shall we exist?* That was the question asked by the early settlers, the Zionists, our grandparents. To be a nation or not a nation, that was the first question for them.

"*With what shall we exist?* That was the question asked by the first-born of the settlers, those that the world knows as the sabras, our parents. They had to build the nation which their parents had decided to create.

"*How shall we exist?* That is the question asked by us, the new generation.

"Our nation has been solidly built. Our state exists and is being defended. We, the new generation, carry on these tasks and take them for granted. But now we are concerned with finding a way to live. We want a normal life, a good job, to raise a family.

"Neither I nor most of my friends would live in a kibbutz, not for a million pounds. To have every step in one's life regulated by a General Assembly! I want to live my life.

"Our forefathers wanted to live their lives, too. That is why they left the Pale of Settlement, the *stetls,* the ghettos of Europe. In their own way, they, too, were highly individualistic. But circumstances forced them to work collectively in very hard times. There was so little they had, they had to share. Thus, the kibbutz, socialism.

"We still have to work together to defend our nation, but in civilian lives we have a right to seek our own ways. We seem, thus, more materialistic, and I suppose we are, because of our circumstances. But we love our Israel, the reality, as much as our parents and grandparents loved Israel, their dream.

"We have an idealism of our own, in our own times.

"I myself have turned down several offers of jobs for very big money, much more than I make. I refused because it was just making money without any social utility. I do have personal ambition, of course, but it is disciplined by and correlated with a sense of service to welfare and to improvement of my profession and of Israeli society.

"I think my newspaper is the best paper in the country.

But I labor to make it better, knowing it will make better-informed citizens and therefore a better, stronger Israel. This motivates my generation. We want a better life both for ourselves and our country, without a lot of ideological and religious nonsense.

"The Zionists say one must come to Israel to be a Jew. I do not believe this. One can be a good Jew, a true Jew, live a Jewish life anywhere, except, of course, in countries where Jews are oppressed.

"In America, there are many good, true Jews. American Jews understand that they need Israel, just as we understand how very much we need America. I like the pressures that American Jews apply to Israel in terms of modernization of our common religion. Without American pressure and examples, the orthodox element would be much more powerful here in Israel. American Jewry is a vital counterbalance.

"America is the social laboratory of the world. What is happening in your country is surely trying, even agonizing for you, but it is the most exciting social test of modern times. America fertilizes the entire world. It may well be the only truly revolutionary country left on earth. The ferment may be be painful but it is good.

"As for Israel, we are the symbol of Jewish sovereignty in the world, of dignity—a dignity enjoyed, through us, by Jews in the Diaspora. If Israel is viable, it means that all Jews are viable.

"Jewishness for us young Israelis does not mean *dovenning;* that is, not ritual. For me, it means a quiet *Shabbat;* it means Challah Friday night. It also means, in a deeper context, a sense of heritage and history, of being descended from great scholars, great teachers. I do not have to stress my Jewishness. That would be like pinning on a yellow star. I take it for granted. I feel Jewish. That is a fact and that is enough.

"We young people would be more religious if established laws were closer to our own way of life. No more nonsense about a Cohen not marrying a divorcée. Or a widow not being able to remarry because her brother-in-law would not release her.

"We believe in the nuclear family. All other theories are simply intellectual exercises. A family is a family—father, mother, and children—with special ties and love.

"Beyond my nuclear family, there is my family of Israel, and beyond that the family of Jews around the world. And beyond that the family of man.

"We are the generation of the fact. We are pragmatic. We are not without higher moral ideals, but first we want to know how to make things work. Not work with our hands because it is noble to work, or to be close to the soil, as our grandparents argued. We work with our hands to make something useful, are close to the soil to grow crops, not for nobility.

"Like our fruit, the sabra, we are prickly outside. We often seem rude, tough. But deep inside we, too, have our conscience, our consciousness of needs beyond our narrow ambitions. But we first ask will it work, not is it good or bad morally. We do not spend an evening arguing about whether there should be a hyphen between labor and Zionist. We like to spend an evening dancing, drinking, enjoying ourselves.

"But when we have to fight, we fight, just as well as the most exalted of our parents and grandparents. Maybe we are not so interesting, so glamorous, so majestic as Ben-Gurion, Meir, and Dayan. This is not an age of heroes. But maybe that's just as well. Heroes are bad administrators. Heroes do not make great diplomats. They can build countries, but can they make them work?

"We, the first Israelis, think we can make Israel work, for Israel and for Jews everywhere, and set an example for the whole world."

*     *     *

We would agree with Gideon Samet that his generation of young Israelis is not a generation of heroes, but it does not necessarily follow that they are not heroic. To yearn for peace but still fight bravely, to plead with medical examiners to ignore physical failings so that the conscript can do his military service—which is what many young Israelis do—this is heroic.

They are not zealots, but that is not a failing.

To say there are no giants among them, no Ben-Gurions, Meirs, or Dayans, may be to say either that the Ben-Gurions, Meirs, and Dayans, by long dominance, have not given young people a chance to show what they can do or, perhaps, that the times do not call for giants. And that is not all bad. We found the first-born citizens of the State of Israel to be essentially sound, healthy, uncomplicated, normal. For a nation whose survival is still at stake, surrounded by hostile neighbors who outnumber them about forty to one, a cool, steady youth is a vital asset.

The new Israelis will not be the last Israelis.

# APPENDIX

## Polls and Analyses of the National Survey

T H E following tables were prepared by Dr. Elie Kenan, staff analyst of the Israeli Institute of Applied Social Research and senior lecturer in political science at the Hebrew University in Jerusalem.

The questions and answers were part of a Continuing Survey of national opinion, conducted quarterly by the Institute. Questions A3, A5, and A9 were asked in the survey of July-August, 1969. D1 and D2 were in the survey of June-July, 1970; November-December, 1970; and October-December, 1971. Questions A2, C1, and E were taken from a special study, "Israeli Culture in 1970," conducted by Professor Elihu Katz in May-July, 1970, based on a sampling of about 4,000 interviewees. The other questions were all based on national samplings of about 2,000 interviewees.

In the breakdown, youth is considered to be under 30 and adults over 30.

A1—In your opinion, are the Arab countries presently disposed to speak about a *real peace* with Israel?

|  | Youth % | Adults % |
|---|---|---|
| Absolutely | 1 | 2 |
| Perhaps | 16 | 18 |
| No, not yet | 66 | 66 |
| Less now than ever | 17 | 14 |
|  | 100 | 100 |

A2—You know, of course, that in Israel there is talk about "hawks" and "doves," the hawks being partisans of a hard line, while the doves are known as those favorable to a conciliatory policy and concessions. How would you classify yourself, on the following scale, in which 1 would represent the most conciliatory position and 9 the hardest line?

|  | Youth % | Adults % |
|---|---|---|
| 1 | 4 | 4 |
| 2 | 2 | 2 |
| 3 | 3 | 5 |
| 4 | 5 | 5 |
| 5 | 19 | 19 |
| 6 | 14 | 14 |
| 7 | 19 | 21 |
| 8 | 14 | 12 |
| 9 | 20 | 18 |
|  | 100 | 100 |

A3—To what extent are you favorable to a harder line for
Israel in respect to the Arab countries?

|  | Youth % | Adults % |
|---|---|---|
| Very favorable | 31 | 32 |
| Favorable to a big extent | 37 | 30 |
| Not so favorable | 20 | 20 |
| Not favorable at all | 12 | 18 |
|  | 100 | 100 |

A4—In the present state of things, do you think that policy
toward the Arab countries should be firmer or more
moderate?

|  | Youth % | Adults % |
|---|---|---|
| Much firmer | 19 | 19 |
| A bit firmer | 27 | 22 |
| Just the way it is now | 43 | 50 |
| A bit more moderate | 10 | 8 |
| Much more moderate | 1 | 1 |
|  | 100 | 100 |

A5—Among various measures, which, in your opinion, is the
best way to reach agreement with the Arabs?

|  | Youth % | Adults % |
|---|---|---|
| Direct negotiations | 88 | 83 |
| U.N. mediation | 4 | 3 |
| Other country mediation | 6 | 7 |
| Other replies | 2 | 7 |
|  | 100 | 100 |

A6—Concerning the territories occupied by Israel since the Six-Day War, which, in your opinion, is the greatest concession to be made to reach a peace agreement with the Arab countries?

|  | Youth % | Adults % |
|---|---|---|
| Give up all the territories | 1 | 1 |
| Give up almost all the territories | 6 | 2 |
| Give up part of the territories | 25 | 28 |
| Give up a small part of the territories | 39 | 40 |
| Don't give up anything at all | 29 | 29 |
|  | 100 | 100 |

A7—In your opinion, should the State of Israel resolve the problem of the Arab refugees of the War of Independence?

|  | Youth % | Adults % |
|---|---|---|
| Yes, absolutely | 9 | 11 |
| I think, yes | 31 | 29 |
| I think, no | 31 | 22 |
| Absolutely not | 29 | 38 |
|  | 100 | 100 |

A8—Concerning Arab refugees who fled their homes during or after the Six-Day War, should the State of Israel authorize them to return home now?

|  | Youth % | Adults % |
|---|---|---|
| Yes, absolutely | 12 | 6 |
| I think, yes | 31 | 24 |
| I think, no | 27 | 25 |
| Absolutely not | 30 | 45 |
|  | 100 | 100 |

A9—What do you think of the manner in which we are presently behaving toward Arabs in the occupied territories?

|  | Youth<br>% | Adults<br>% |
|---|---|---|
| We are behaving much too well | 39 | 40 |
| Perhaps too well | 31 | 26 |
| Just what it should be | 27 | 33 |
| Perhaps not so well | 2 | 1 |
| Not well at all | 1 | — |
|  | 100 | 100 |

A10—Would you be prepared to accept an Arab as a friend?

|  | Youth<br>% | Adults<br>% |
|---|---|---|
| Yes, absolutely | 30 | 31 |
| That would depend upon<br>circumstances | 42 | 32 |
| No | 12 | 17 |
| Absolutely not | 16 | 20 |
|  | 100 | 100 |

## INTERNAL QUESTIONS

B1—Transfer of a part of the defense budget to the social welfare budget

Some believe that in present circumstances the government should transfer funds from the defense budget (without endangering the purchase of military equipment) to the budgets for housing, social services, and aid to the most disadvantaged sectors of the population; others argue that this is not the time to effect such a transfer. What is your opinion?

|  | Youth % | Adults % |
|---|---|---|
| It is absolutely necessary to transfer funds from the defense budget to the budgets for housing and social aid | 25 | 13 |
| Perhaps such a transfer should be carried out | 33 | 21 |
| Perhaps such a transfer should not be carried out | 12 | 13 |
| We must not make such a transfer | 30 | 53 |
|  | 100 | 100 |

B2—Intercommunity relations

There exist several communities in Israel, such as the Ashkenazim and the Sephardim. In your opinion, are relations between those communities good at the present time?

|  | Youth % | Adults % |
|---|---|---|
| Very good | 4 | 5 |
| Good enough | 37 | 43 |
| Not very good | 46 | 41 |
| Not good at all | 13 | 11 |
|  | 100 | 100 |

B3—Relations between religious and nonreligious citizens

There exist divergent opinions among Jews on the problem of religion in Israel. Do you think that at present relations between religious and nonreligious Jews are good?

|  | Youth % | Adults % |
|---|---|---|
| Very good | 1 | 3 |
| Good enough | 10 | 17 |
| Not so good | 54 | 51 |
| Not good at all | 35 | 29 |
|  | 100 | 100 |

B4—The practice of religion

Do you customarily observe Jewish tradition?

|  | Youth % | Adults % |
|---|---|---|
| Yes, absolutely; I try to observe it in detail | 10 | 15 |
| I try to observe most religious tradition | 8 | 12 |
| I observe Jewish tradition in part | 46 | 47 |
| I do not observe Jewish tradition at all | 36 | 26 |
|  | 100 | 100 |

C—Judgments on democracy, government, and governmental policy

C1—Imagine that position 1 on the scale represents a situation of total lack of democracy—that is, a dictatorship (of an individual or a group)—and that position 9 represents a very advanced form of democracy. Where, in your opinion, would you place Israel on such a scale?

|  | Youth % | Adults % |
|---|---|---|
| 1 } 2 | 1 | 1 |
| 3 | 1 | 1 |
| 4 | 2 | 2 |
| 5 | 6 | 9 |
| 6 | 11 | 11 |
| 7 | 24 | 24 |
| 8 | 29 | 22 |
| 9 | 26 | 30 |
|  | 100 | 100 |

C2—In your opinion, should the people of Israel identify with their government more than people do in other democratic countries?

|                    | Youth | Adults |
|--------------------|-------|--------|
|                    | %     | %      |
| Yes, absolutely    | 39    | 49     |
| Perhaps yes        | 33    | 29     |
| Perhaps no         | 12    | 10     |
| Absolutely not     | 16    | 12     |
|                    | 100   | 100    |

C3—To what extent is it important for you to criticize governmental action when you do not approve of it?

|                     | Youth | Adults |
|---------------------|-------|--------|
|                     | %     | %      |
| Very important      | 25    | 19     |
| Important enough     | 46    | 46     |
| Not so important    | 21    | 21     |
| Not important at all | 8     | 14     |
|                     | 100   | 100    |

C4—What do you think of the way government is handling present problems?

|                 | Youth | Adults |
|-----------------|-------|--------|
|                 | %     | %      |
| Very good       | 3     | 9      |
| Good enough     | 45    | 54     |
| Not so good     | 44    | 31     |
| Not at all good | 8     | 6      |
|                 | 100   | 100    |

C5—What do you think of the way government is handling each of the following problems?

| 1. *The Country's Security* | Youth | Adults |
|-----------------------------|-------|--------|
|                             | %     | %      |
| Very successfully           | 26    | 32     |
| Successfully                | 68    | 64     |

|  | Youth % | Adults % |
|---|---|---|
| Not so successfully | 5 | 3 |
| Not successfully | 1 | — |
| Not at all successfully | — | 1 |
|  | 100 | 100 |

## 2. *Relations with Other Countries*

|  | Youth | Adults |
|---|---|---|
| Very successfully | 8 | 11 |
| Successfully | 58 | 59 |
| Not so successfully | 28 | 25 |
| Not successfully | 4 | 3 |
| Not at all successfully | 2 | 2 |
|  | 100 | 100 |

## 3. *The Nation's Economy*

|  | Youth | Adults |
|---|---|---|
| Very successfully | 2 | 3 |
| Successfully | 19 | 26 |
| Not so successfully | 32 | 27 |
| Not successfully | 36 | 34 |
| Not at all successfully | 11 | 10 |
|  | 100 | 100 |

D—Morale before and after the cease-fire of August, 1970

D1—Are you worried these days?

|  | June-July 1970 Y. | June-July 1970 A. | Nov.-Dec. 1970 Y. | Nov.-Dec. 1970 A. | Oct.-Nov. 1971 Y. | Oct.-Nov. 1971 A. |
|---|---|---|---|---|---|---|
|  | % | | % | | % | |
| Always | 9 | 19 | 5 | 14 | 6 | 12 |
| Almost always | 10 | 15 | 6 | 10 | 6 | 11 |
| Often | 24 | 27 | 15 | 17 | 16 | 18 |
| Sometimes | 36 | 31 | 46 | 43 | 43 | 40 |
| Almost never / Never | 21 | 8 | 28 | 16 | 29 | 19 |
|  | 100 | 100 | 100 | 100 | 100 | 100 |

D2—To what extent do each of the following questions cause you concern?

1. *Israel's Security*

| | Youth % | Adults % |
|---|---|---|
| Much concern | 26 | 33 |
| Some concern | 50 | 45 |
| Not much concern | 13 | 11 |
| No concern | 9 | 7 |
| No concern at all | 2 | 4 |
| | 100 | 100 |

2. *The Political Situation in Israel*

| | | |
|---|---|---|
| Much concern | 14 | 19 |
| Some concern | 49 | 52 |
| Not much concern | 24 | 18 |
| No concern | 9 | 8 |
| No concern at all | 4 | 3 |
| | 100 | 100 |

3. *The Economic Situation in Israel*

| | | |
|---|---|---|
| Much concern | 17 | 20 |
| Some concern | 56 | 55 |
| Not much concern | 19 | 15 |
| No concern | 6 | 8 |
| No concern at all | 2 | 2 |
| | 100 | 100 |

4. *The War-Making Ability of the Israeli Army*

| | | |
|---|---|---|
| Much concern | 14 | 17 |
| Some concern | 14 | 18 |
| Not much concern | 12 | 11 |
| No concern | 29 | 27 |
| No concern at all | 31 | 27 |
| | 100 | 100 |

E—The memory of European Jews exterminated by the Nazis

E1—Are you preoccupied by the extermination of the Jews of Europe (the fact that six million were exterminated by the Nazis)?

|  | Youth | Adults |
|---|---|---|
|  | % | % |
| Very often | 9 | 36 |
| Often | 36 | 34 |
| Rarely | 38 | 21 |
| Very rarely | 12 | 6 |
| Not at all | 5 | 3 |
|  | 100 | 100 |

# INDEX

DAVID SCHOENBRUN, long-time chief correspondent for CBS News, author of best-selling books on France, de Gaulle, and Vietnam, has reported on Israel in world affairs for the past twenty years. He has won major awards in every field of communications—radio reporting, television reporting, books on foreign affairs, magazine articles, and has been named commentator of the year. A senior lecturer at Columbia University and at the New School for Social Research, he is that rarity, a hard-hitting reporter and respected scholar.

ROBERT SZEKELY is an economist and analyst for Euro-Finance, a Paris-based research organization, the largest and most distinguished organization in its field in Europe. Born in Budapest, in 1945, he emigrated to America, and took his undergraduate work at NYU and his master's at Columbia University's School of International Affairs.

LUCY SZEKELY, born in Paris in 1947, took her baccalaureate in Paris and her university degree in languages and history at NYU. She has worked as French broadcaster for United Nations Radio, researcher and assistant producer for ABC-TV News in New York and ORTF, the French National Television Network, in Paris.